Title: "Quantum Insights: Navigati

ng

Develop

mental

Stages

through

AI Time Travel "

Table Of contents:

Chapter 1: The Quantum Prelude
Introduction to Quantum Machine Learning (QML) and its Mystical Capabilities.

Chapter 2: Unraveling Time Threads
Understanding the concept of time travel in the context of AI and Quantum Computing.

Chapter 3: Simulating the Cosmos *Exploring the integration of AI and QML for simulating entire sectors and their developmental stages.*

Chapter 4: The Quantum Code of Life
Applying QML to decode the stages of individual and societal development.

Chapter 5: The Birth of Sectors *Quantum insights into the inception and infancy of sectors through advanced simulations.*

Chapter 6: Toddler Steps in Technology *AI-driven analyses of the initial strides taken by technology sectors.*

Chapter 7: The Adolescence of Industry *Exploring the rebellious yet transformative phases in industrial development through QML.*

Chapter 8: Quantum Maturation of Finance *Understanding financial sectors and their quantum evolution over time.*

Chapter 9: Simulated Wisdom in Healthcare *AI-guided journey through the stages of development in the healthcare industry.*

Chapter 10: Quantum Agriculture Revolution *Using QML to predict and enhance agricultural advancements.*

Chapter 11: Quantum Threads of Energy
Simulating energy sectors and their transitions with AI and quantum computing.

Chapter 12: Cosmic Connectivity in Communication Examining how communication sectors evolve in the cosmic simulation.

Chapter 13: AI and Quantum Culture Craft
Quantum insights into the cultural evolution of societies through AI-driven simulations.

Chapter 14: The Quantum Era of Education
Navigating the simulated realms of education and its quantum transformations.

Chapter 15: Virtualization of Reality Blurring the lines between reality and simulation using AI and quantum technologies.

Chapter 16: AI in the Quantum Political Arena Analyzing the political stages of development through the lens of quantum-powered AI.

Chapter 17: Quantum Transport and Connectivity *Simulating the evolution of transportation and connectivity sectors.*

Chapter 18: The Quantum Pulse of Environment *Detecting environmental changes and developmental stages through AI-enhanced simulations.*

Chapter 19: Quantum Exploration of Quantum Research *AI-driven insights into the stages of development in the field of scientific research.*

Chapter 20: The Future Unveiled *Peering into the future using quantum machine learning, discussing its potentials and ethical considerations.*

Chapter 21: Quantum Reflections *A holistic reflection on the mystical journey through developmental stages using AI, quantum machine learning, and simulated time travel.*

Chapter 1: The Quantum Prelude

As the sun dipped below the horizon, casting hues of orange and violet across the landscape, a group of researchers gathered in a dimly lit room, surrounded by humming quantum computers. Among them were Dr. Evelyn Mercer, a seasoned quantum physicist, and Dr. Oliver Stone, an enthusiastic AI specialist. The air buzzed with anticipation.

Dr. Mercer: (leaning over a holographic display) Today marks the beginning of our journey into the quantum realm, where the rules of classical computing bend, and new possibilities emerge.

Dr. Stone: (adjusting his glasses) Quantum Machine Learning... the very phrase carries an air of mystique. What secrets does it hold?

Alice: (a young researcher, wide-eyed) Are we talking about time travel? Like in the movies?

Dr. Mercer: (smiling) Not quite, Alice. But we are delving into a domain where machines, guided by the principles of quantum mechanics, can unlock insights beyond our classical understanding.

Bob: *(a seasoned programmer)* So, how does Quantum Machine Learning differ from classical methods?

Dr. Stone: *(nodding)* In classical computing, data is processed using bits—either 0 or 1. But in quantum computing, we leverage qubits, which can exist in multiple states simultaneously, thanks to superposition and entanglement.

Eva: *(a quantum enthusiast)* So, it's like exploring multiple possibilities at once?

Dr. Mercer: Precisely, Eva. It's as if we're dancing on the threads of different timelines.

As the conversation unfolded, the room resonated with the hum of the quantum processors, creating an ambiance that felt both futuristic and ancient.

Dr. Stone: *(typing on a holographic keyboard)* Quantum Machine Learning allows us to *process and analyze vast amounts of data, exploring intricate patterns that classical algorithms might overlook.*

Alice: *(intrigued) So, we're not just dealing with 0s and 1s anymore?*

Dr. Mercer: *No, Alice. Qubits can be 0, 1, or any quantum superposition of these states. It's a dance of probabilities.*

Bob: *(scratching his head) But how does this help us understand development stages?*

Dr. Stone: *(smirking) That's where the magic happens. Imagine we're not just predicting outcomes; we're creating a symphony of possibilities, each note representing a potential developmental stage.*

The holographic display flickered, revealing a complex web of interconnected nodes and pathways.

Eva: *(whispering) It's beautiful.*

Dr. Mercer: *(gesturing at the hologram) In this quantum symphony, we can simulate the evolution of systems over time. It's not just prediction; it's comprehension on a cosmic scale.*

The team spent hours immersed in dialogue, discussing quantum entanglement, algorithmic symphonies, and the mystical dance of qubits. As the night deepened, the quantum processors continued their silent calculations, as if echoing the vastness of the quantum realm.

Alice: *(looking at the holographic display) So, this is where our journey begins?*

Dr. Stone: *(nodding) Indeed, Alice. Our journey into the quantum prelude—a realm where the symphony of possibilities orchestrates the understanding of developmental stages in ways we've never imagined.*

And with that, the room embraced the enigmatic hum of quantum processors, setting the stage for a journey into the unknown, where quantum mysteries and machine learning entwined in a dance of exploration.

Chapter 2: Unravelin

g Time Threads

The research facility hummed with a peculiar energy as Dr. Evelyn Mercer and Dr. Oliver Stone continued their exploration into the realm of quantum possibilities. The air seemed charged with anticipation as the team gathered, ready to unravel the enigma of time threads entwined with AI and quantum computing.

Dr. Mercer: *(addressing the team) Our journey takes a quantum leap into the concept of time travel. Not the kind you see in movies with flux capacitors and DeLoreans, but a voyage through the threads of possibilities, guided by the principles of quantum mechanics.*

Dr. Stone: *(projecting a holographic timeline)* Picture time not as a linear path, but as a vast web of interconnected threads. Each decision, each event, creates a branching in these threads, leading to an infinite array of potential futures.

Alice: *(intrigued) So, are we going back to the past or into the future?*

Dr. Mercer: *(smiling) In a way, both. Quantum computing allows us to process information in ways that mimic the fluidity of time. We're not stepping into a time machine, but rather, we're navigating the time threads that weave through the quantum fabric.*

Bob: *(raising an eyebrow) How does AI fit into this temporal tapestry?*

Dr. Stone: *Excellent question, Bob. AI becomes our guide, our navigator through the intricate patterns of time. By leveraging quantum algorithms, we empower AI to discern the potential consequences of various decisions, to forecast and simulate the future.*

As the holographic timeline flickered, images of branching threads and converging possibilities painted an ethereal picture of the interconnectedness of time.

Eva: (pointing at a branching node) What happens when a decision splits the timeline?

Dr. Mercer: (nodding) Ah, the essence of quantum superposition. When a decision is made, the timeline splits, creating a multitude of parallel universes. AI helps us explore these divergent paths, understanding the unfolding of events in each thread.

Alice: (whispering) It's like playing a cosmic chess game.

Dr. Stone: (chuckling) Indeed, Alice. The pieces are decisions, and the board is the fabric of time itself.

The team engaged in a lively discussion, dissecting the intricacies of quantum superposition, entanglement, and the role of AI as the temporal guide. The holographic timeline evolved, showcasing the team's collective understanding of the quantum prelude they had just embarked upon.

Bob: (leaning back) So, we're not just observers; we're active participants in shaping these time threads?

Dr. Mercer: (smirking) Precisely, Bob. As we simulate, predict, and understand the consequences of our actions, we become weavers of the cosmic tapestry, shaping the very threads of time.

The holographic display pulsed with an otherworldly glow, as if reflecting the pulsating heartbeat of time itself.

Eva: (softly) It's mesmerizing, yet humbling.

Dr. Stone: (looking at the hologram) Indeed, Eva. Our journey is not just about understanding time; it's about coexisting with its infinite possibilities.

As the team delved deeper into the intricacies of time threads, the quantum processors hummed *in harmony, forging a connection between AI, quantum computing, and the timeless mysteries that awaited them in the chapters yet to unfold. The symphony of possibilities echoed through the research facility, a testament to the team's quest to unravel the threads that bound them to the quantum prelude of time.*

Chapter 3: Simulatin

g the
Cosmos

The research facility's quantum processors hummed with anticipation as Dr. Evelyn Mercer and Dr. Oliver Stone embarked on a journey to simulate entire sectors, unraveling the cosmos with the integration of Artificial Intelligence (AI) and Quantum Machine Learning (QML). In a room filled with the soft glow of holographic displays, the team prepared to dive into the intricate dance between algorithms and quantum mechanics.

Dr. Mercer: *(addressing the team) Today, we embark on a grand expedition—simulating entire sectors, from the microcosms of technology to the vast expanses of industries,* using the unparalleled capabilities of AI and Quantum Machine Learning.

Dr. Stone: (gesturing to the holographic displays) The cosmos we're about to explore isn't limited to the celestial. It encompasses the intricate web of interconnected sectors that shape our reality.

Alice: (excitedly) Are we creating a virtual universe?

Dr. Mercer: (smiling) In a sense, Alice. Our universe will be one of data, algorithms, and quantum entanglements.

The team gathered around the holographic displays, each researcher eager to witness the birth of a simulated cosmos.

Dr. Stone: (typing commands) Let's start small—simulating the technology sector. AI, powered by Quantum Machine Learning, will unravel patterns, predict developments, and guide us through the stages of technological evolution.

The holographic display flickered, and a virtual representation of the technology sector materialized—a pulsating, ethereal landscape of code and algorithms.

Bob: *(raising an eyebrow) How does this simulation differ from conventional modeling?*

Dr. Mercer: *(explaining) Conventional models are confined by the limitations of classical computing, unable to capture the quantum nature of reality. With QML, we leverage the quantum realm to process vast datasets and simulate the intricate relationships within sectors.*

Eva: *(pointing at the hologram) It's like peering into the future of technology.*

Dr. Stone: *(nodding) Indeed, Eva. Now, let's broaden our canvas. We'll simulate not just one sector, but an entire ecosystem—technology, finance, healthcare, interwoven like a cosmic tapestry.*

As Dr. Stone initiated the simulation, the holographic display expanded, revealing a vast interconnected network of sectors, each node pulsating with the rhythm of simulated development.

Alice: (whispering) It's like watching the birth of a digital universe.

Dr. Mercer: (voice filled with awe) Our cosmos is expanding—each algorithmic interaction, every simulated decision, shaping the destiny of these sectors.

The team engaged in animated discussions, deciphering the quantum algorithms orchestrating the cosmic dance unfolding before them.

Bob: (intrigued) How does AI adapt to the quantum nature of the simulation?

Dr. Stone: (explaining) In this cosmos, AI isn't bound by deterministic pathways. Quantum algorithms allow AI to navigate the vast *possibilities, adapting to the fluidity of quantum superposition and entanglement.*

Eva: *(gazing at the hologram) Can we simulate the impact of a technological breakthrough on other sectors?*

Dr. Mercer: *(smirking) That's the beauty of our cosmos. Let's introduce a quantum leap in technology and observe its cascading effects.*

As the team simulated the breakthrough, the holographic display rippled with changes—a surge in technological advancements influencing finance, healthcare, and every interconnected sector.

Alice: *(wide-eyed) It's like playing a celestial symphony, with each note resonating across the cosmos.*

Dr. Stone: *(looking at the display with pride) Our journey doesn't end here. We'll continue exploring, simulating, and unraveling the mysteries of developmental stages across* sectors, guided by the harmonious convergence of AI and Quantum Machine Learning.

The holographic cosmos continued to evolve, a testament to the team's endeavor to push the boundaries of understanding. In the quantum prelude of simulation, they glimpsed the vast potential of AI and QML—a cosmic dance that transcended the limits of conventional modeling and opened doors to a new frontier of exploration.

Chapter 4: The

Quantum Code of Life

In the heart of the research facility, where the glow of quantum processors met the fervor of intellectual curiosity, Dr. Evelyn Mercer and Dr. Oliver Stone set out on an extraordinary expedition. Their mission: to unravel the quantum code that underlies the stages of both individual and societal development, employing the enigmatic powers of Quantum Machine Learning (QML).

Dr. Mercer: *(addressing the team) Today, we embark on a journey that delves into the very fabric of existence—the quantum code that shapes the intricate dance of life.*

Dr. Stone: *(with a gleam in his eye) The Quantum Code of Life is not written in strings of DNA alone; it resonates in the collective choices of individuals and societies, waiting to be deciphered.*

Alice: *(curious) Are we decoding our own destinies?*

Dr. Mercer: *(smiling) Indeed, Alice. The quantum code we seek intertwines the destinies of individuals and the trajectories of entire societies.*

The team gathered around holographic displays, eager to witness the unveiling of the quantum code.

Dr. Stone: *(activating the displays) Let's start with the individual—a microcosm of choices, experiences, and potentialities. QML will guide* *us through the stages of personal development, decoding the quantum signatures that define our journeys.*

The holographic display shimmered, revealing intricate patterns that mirrored the complexities of an individual's life.

Bob: *(scratching his head) How can we quantify personal development in terms of quantum mechanics?*

Dr. Mercer: *(explaining) In the quantum realm, possibilities exist in superposition. Similarly, an individual's choices create a superposition of potential life paths. QML analyzes these possibilities, offering insights into the stages of personal development.*

As the team delved into the quantum signatures of personal development, the holographic display unfolded a tapestry of choices, experiences, and transformative moments.

Eva: *(mesmerized) It's like mapping the very essence of our existence.*

Dr. Stone: *(nodding) Now, let's extend our gaze to societal development. The quantum code that shapes cultures, norms, and the collective evolution of civilizations.*

The holographic display expanded, revealing a complex interplay of societal elements— economies, governance, cultural dynamics—all entwined in the quantum dance.

Alice: *(with a hint of awe) Can we predict societal shifts, like paradigm changes or revolutions?*

Dr. Mercer: *(smirking) The quantum code allows us to anticipate the rippling effects of collective choices. Let's introduce a societal catalyst and observe the quantum signatures of change.*

As the team simulated a societal catalyst, the holographic display responded with a cascade of transformations—a visual representation of how collective decisions could reshape the quantum code of societal development.

Bob: (captivated) It's like playing with the threads that weave the fabric of civilization.

Dr. Stone: (musing) Indeed, Bob. Our journey into the Quantum Code of Life is a quest to understand the intricate interplay between individual choices and societal evolution.

The team engaged in deep discussions, exploring the quantum entanglements that bind personal and societal development. They dissected the complexities of quantum algorithms that could decode the very essence of life's progression.

Eva: (reflecting) How does ethical behavior fit into this quantum tapestry?

Dr. Mercer: (serious) Ethical considerations are the guiding stars in our journey. QML not only helps us understand development but also emphasizes the importance of responsible choices at both individual and societal levels.

As the holographic display continued to evolve, Dr. Mercer and Dr. Stone realized that the

Quantum Code of Life was not merely an exploration of possibilities but a call for ethical contemplation in the face of quantum potentials.

Alice: (softly) It's not just about understanding; it's about shaping a conscious quantum existence.

Dr. Stone: (nodding) Our exploration doesn't end here. The Quantum Code of Life beckons us to delve deeper into the mysteries that bind us to the very essence of our existence.

As the quantum processors hummed in symphony with the team's contemplation, they stood at the threshold of a profound understanding—the quantum code that intricately weaved the stages of life, both individual and societal, into a mesmerizing dance of potentialities. The quantum prelude of existence unfolded, inviting them to decipher the enigmatic script that lay at the heart of the Quantum Code of Life.

Chapter 5: The Birth of Sectors

In the heart of the research facility, where the pulse of quantum processors met the fervor of exploration, Dr. Evelyn Mercer and Dr. Oliver Stone embarked on a fascinating odyssey—a journey into the quantum insights that unveil the inception and infancy of sectors. The team gathered, eager to witness the birth of sectors through the lens of advanced simulations and quantum revelations.

Dr. Mercer: (addressing the team) Today, we venture into the primordial quantum soup, seeking insights into the birthing cries of sectors—those entities that shape the very fabric of our societal existence.

Dr. Stone: (with a spark of enthusiasm) The birth of sectors is not a mundane event; it's a quantum symphony, and we are here to decode its harmonies.

Alice: (intrigued) Are we witnessing the creation of industries from scratch?

Dr. Mercer: (nodding) Indeed, Alice. Through Quantum Machine Learning, we will not only witness but actively participate in the quantum birth of sectors, understanding how choices, innovations, and societal needs intertwine.

The team assembled around holographic displays, ready to peer into the quantum crucible where sectors are conceived.

Dr. Stone: (activating simulations) Let's start with the genesis of the technology sector—a realm where ideas spark, innovations ignite, and possibilities flourish.

The holographic display materialized a digital canvas, a blank slate pulsating with quantum potential.

Bob: (questioning) How do we simulate the birth of an industry in a quantum context?

Dr. Mercer: (explaining) In quantum simulations, possibilities are not predefined; they emerge from the superposition of potential states. By introducing quantum uncertainties into our models, we can simulate the organic emergence of sectors.

As the quantum algorithms danced across the holographic canvas, patterns began to emerge—potential innovations, technological breakthroughs, and the quantum signatures of a burgeoning sector.

Eva: (captivated) It's like watching the universe unfold.

Dr. Stone: (smiling) Precisely, Eva. Now, let's broaden our scope. We'll simulate not just one sector but a symphony of intertwined industries—finance, healthcare, energy—all emerging from the quantum crucible.

The holographic display expanded, revealing a cosmic ballet of sectors, each one evolving in harmony with the quantum fluctuations.

Alice: (astounded) Can we influence the direction these sectors take?

Dr. Mercer: (intrigued) A question at the heart of our exploration. Quantum simulations allow us to introduce catalysts—innovations, economic shifts, or societal changes—and observe their quantum echoes on sectoral evolution.

The team engaged in discussions, orchestrating quantum simulations that mimicked the emergence of sectors under various influences.

Bob: (pointing at the hologram) What happens when sectors collide or influence each other?

Dr. Stone: (chuckling) Ah, the dance of intersectoral dynamics. Let's introduce a scenario where technological advancements in one sector catalyze innovations in others.

As the team manipulated the quantum parameters, the holographic display responded with a breathtaking display of interconnected sectors—each one influencing and shaping the developmental trajectory of the others.

Eva: (musing) It's not just about the birth of sectors; it's about their interconnected destinies.

Dr. Mercer: (reflecting) Indeed, Eva. The quantum birth of sectors is not isolated but part of a grand tapestry where each thread contributes to the fabric of societal evolution.

As the holographic display continued to evolve, the team realized they were not mere observers but active participants in the cosmic ballet of sectoral birth and evolution.

Alice: (softly) Are we creators in this quantum symphony?

Dr. Stone: (with a contemplative gaze) In a way, Alice. By understanding and influencing the quantum dynamics of sectoral birth, we become architects of the future, shaping the destiny of industries yet to emerge.

The quantum processors hummed in harmony with the team's reflections, resonating with the symphony of potentialities that unfolded before them. The birth of sectors, a quantum spectacle, beckoned the researchers to explore further—to unravel the mysteries of quantum birth and the cosmic dance that shapes the very foundation of societal existence.

Chapter 6: Toddler

Steps in Technology

In the pulsating heart of the research facility, where the hum of quantum processors met the brilliance of artificial intelligence, Dr. Evelyn Mercer and Dr. Oliver Stone embarked on a journey to explore the toddler steps of technology sectors. The team gathered, eager to witness the AI-driven analyses of the initial strides taken by the burgeoning technologies— those infantile footsteps that would eventually shape the landscapes of industries and societies.

Dr. Mercer: *(addressing the team) Today, we delve into the early chapters of technological evolution, where innovations take their first, tentative steps—the toddler phase of technology sectors.*

Dr. Stone: *(with an air of excitement) The infancy of technology is a playground of potentialities, and through the lens of AI, we shall unravel the nuances of these early strides.*

Alice: *(curious) Are we going back in time to witness the beginnings of technologies?*

Dr. Mercer: *(smiling) Not quite, Alice. Through Quantum Machine Learning and advanced AI analyses, we shall simulate and understand the foundational moments that propel technology sectors into existence.*

The team converged around holographic displays, ready to witness the AI-driven analyses that would unfold the technological toddlerhood.

Dr. Stone: *(activating simulations) Let's begin with a classic—personal computing. A sector that took its first steps not too long ago, yet reshaped the way we live and work.*

The holographic display conjured images of vintage computers, lines of code, and the birth of a sector that would revolutionize the world.

Bob: *(intrigued) How can AI help us analyze the early stages of technology?*

Dr. Mercer: *(explaining) AI acts as our temporal lens, allowing us to analyze historical data, predict emerging trends, and simulate the developmental trajectory of technology sectors. It's like watching the past with the eyes of the future.*

As the team engaged in discussions, the holographic display unfolded the toddler steps of personal computing—moments of innovation, breakthroughs, and the early market dynamics.

Eva: *(captivated) It's like we're witnessing the infancy of our digital age.*

Dr. Stone: *(nodding) Now, let's broaden our scope. We'll explore the toddlerhood of not just one sector but a medley of emerging technologies—artificial intelligence, blockchain, biotechnology—all taking their first strides.*

The holographic display expanded, revealing a dynamic landscape of intertwining technologies—each one a toddler taking its own, unique steps.

Alice: *(questioning) Can we predict which technologies will thrive and which will face challenges?*

Dr. Mercer: *(smirking) A question that fuels our exploration. Through AI-driven analyses, we can introduce scenarios, simulate potential obstacles, and gauge the resilience of technologies in their early stages.*

As the team manipulated the quantum parameters, the holographic display responded with scenarios of success, challenges, and the unpredictable twists that characterized the toddlerhood of emerging technologies.

Bob: (pointing at the hologram) How do societal factors influence the growth of these technological toddlers?

Dr. Stone: (acknowledging) An excellent point, Bob. Let's introduce societal shifts—economic changes, cultural influences—and observe their impact on the developmental trajectories of these technologies.

The holographic display evolved, depicting the symbiotic dance between societal factors and the strides of technological toddlers.

Eva: (contemplative) It's not just about the technologies; it's about the dance between innovation and the world that nurtures it.

Dr. Mercer: (reflecting) Indeed, Eva. The toddler steps in technology are not isolated events but part of a grand narrative where societal *dynamics and technological evolution intertwine.*

As the holographic display continued to unfold the technological toddlerhood, the team realized that these early steps were not just about innovation; they were about resilience, adaptability, and the intricate dance between human ingenuity and the societal fabric.

Alice: *(softly) Are we shaping the future as we analyze the past?*

Dr. Stone: *(with a knowing smile) In a way, Alice. Our analyses, simulations, and insights become guiding stars for the technology sectors yet to take their first steps. We are not just observers; we are stewards of the technological future.*

The quantum processors hummed in resonance with the team's contemplation, echoing the synergistic dance between AI, quantum insights, and the toddler steps of technology sectors. The journey into the technological past unveiled not only the infancy of innovation but also the profound impact these early strides would have on the future technological tapestry.

Chapter 7: The

Adolescence of Industry

In the hallowed halls of the research facility, where the hum of quantum processors blended with the intellectual fervor, Dr. Evelyn Mercer and Dr. Oliver Stone embarked on an extraordinary exploration. The team gathered, ready to journey into the rebellious yet transformative phases of industrial development—an exploration guided by Quantum Machine Learning (QML), where the adolescent industries carve their unique path toward maturity.

Dr. Mercer: (addressing the team) Today, we venture into the tumultuous stages of industrial adolescence—a time of rebellion, transformation, and the forging of identities that will resonate through the ages.

Dr. Stone: (with a spark in his eyes) The adolescence of industry is a canvas of innovation, disruption, and resilience. Through QML, we shall unravel the quantum signatures that define this rebellious phase.

Alice: (curious) Are we diving into historical industrial revolutions?

Dr. Mercer: (smiling) Not just historical, Alice. We're using QML to simulate and understand the rebellious journeys of industries—past, present, and those on the cusp of transformation.

The team gathered around holographic displays, eager to witness the adolescence of industries unfold through the quantum lens.

Dr. Stone: *(activating simulations) Let's commence with an iconic example—the Industrial Revolution. A period that shook the foundations of society, marking the rebellious adolescence of industries.*

The holographic display flickered, bringing to life the smoke-filled factories, clanking machinery, and the birth of a new industrial era.

Bob: *(inquiring) How does QML help us analyze the rebellious phases of industries?*

Dr. Mercer: *(explaining) QML allows us to process vast amounts of historical data, simulate the impact of various factors, and predict the trajectories of industries during their formative years. It's akin to having a quantum crystal ball that reveals the rebellious dance of innovation.*

As the team engaged in discussions, the holographic display unveiled the tumultuous adolescence of the Industrial Revolution—

innovations, societal shifts, and the quantum echoes of transformation.

Eva: *(captivated)* It's like witnessing the birth pangs of modern civilization.

Dr. Stone: *(nodding)* Now, let's extend our gaze to more recent industrial upheavals. We'll explore sectors like information technology, biotechnology, and renewable energy, each undergoing its own rebellious adolescence.

The holographic display expanded, revealing a dynamic landscape of industries in their adolescent rebellion—disruptive startups, paradigm shifts, and the quantum footprints of innovation.

Alice: *(questioning)* Can we predict which industries will lead the next wave of transformation?

Dr. Mercer: *(smirking)* A question that defines our quest. Through QML, we can introduce hypothetical scenarios, simulate emerging trends, and predict the quantum trajectories of industries on the brink of transformative adolescence.

As the team manipulated the quantum parameters, the holographic display responded with scenarios of potential industrial revolutions—each one a rebellious spark in the adolescence of industry.

Bob: (pointing at the hologram) How do global events, like economic recessions or pandemics, influence this rebellious phase?

Dr. Stone: (acknowledging) An astute observation, Bob. Let's introduce external factors and observe their quantum impact on the rebellious journeys of industries.

The holographic display evolved, depicting the interplay between external shocks and the resilient response of industries in their adolescent rebellions.

Eva: (contemplative) It's not just about innovation; it's about how industries navigate adversity during their formative years.

Dr. Mercer: *(reflecting) Indeed, Eva. The adolescence of industry is not just a phase of rebellion; it's a transformative journey where industries shape and are shaped by the world around them.*

As the holographic display continued to unfold the rebellious adolescence, the team realized that these phases were not mere chaotic disruptions; they were the crucibles where industries forged their identities, resilience, and the potential to redefine the fabric of societies.

Alice: *(softly) Are we witnesses to the birth of future civilizations?*

Dr. Stone: *(with a profound gaze) In a way, Alice. The adolescence of industry is a pivotal chapter, and our analyses become a compass guiding industries toward maturity. We are not just witnesses; we are chroniclers of the quantum rebellions that define the industrial landscapes of tomorrow.*

The quantum processors hummed in resonance with the team's reflections, echoing the rebellious spirit of industries navigating their adolescent phases. The exploration into the tumultuous journey of industrial adolescence was not just an analysis of the past; it was a visionary quest to understand the quantum footprints that would shape the industries of the future.

Chapter 8: Quantum

Maturation of Finance

In the sanctum of the research facility, where the rhythm of quantum processors intertwined with the pulse of financial data, Dr. Evelyn Mercer and Dr. Oliver Stone embarked on a profound exploration. The team assembled, ready to unravel the intricate journey of the financial sectors—a journey guided by the enigmatic forces of Quantum Machine Learning (QML) that govern the quantum maturation of finance over time.

Dr. Mercer: *(addressing the team) Today, we immerse ourselves in the quantum evolution of finance—a realm where every transaction, every innovation, leaves a quantum footprint on the fabric of our economic landscapes.*

Dr. Stone: *(with a contemplative demeanor) The maturation of finance is not merely a linear progression; it's a dance of quantum probabilities, shaped by innovations, crises, and the collective choices of societies.*

Alice: *(intrigued) Are we decoding the financial history of the world?*

Dr. Mercer: *(smiling) Indeed, Alice. Through Quantum Machine Learning, we shall simulate and understand the quantum maturation of finance—tracing its footsteps from the earliest financial systems to the complex, interconnected networks we navigate today.*

The team gathered around holographic displays, poised to witness the quantum evolution of finance unfold through the quantum lens.

Dr. Stone: *(activating simulations) Let's commence our journey with the inception of modern banking systems—an era where ledger books and handwritten transactions laid the foundation for what we now know as finance.*

The holographic display flickered to life, revealing the archaic ledgers and the birth of financial institutions that would shape the course of history.

Bob: *(inquiring) How can QML help us understand the historical evolution of finance?*

Dr. Mercer: *(explaining) QML allows us to analyze vast datasets, simulate the impact of financial innovations, and predict the quantum trajectories of financial sectors. It's like unfolding the pages of history with a quantum quill.*

As the team engaged in discussions, the holographic display unveiled the early stages of financial maturation—barter systems evolving into currencies, the birth of stock exchanges, and the quantum echoes of economic revolutions.

Eva: *(captivated) It's like witnessing the birth of capitalism itself.*

Dr. Stone: *(nodding) Now, let's fast forward to more recent times. We'll explore the quantum maturation of finance through key milestones— global economic shifts, the rise of technology, and the birth of novel financial instruments.*

The holographic display expanded, revealing a dynamic landscape of financial evolution— trading floors, digital transactions, and the quantum signatures of maturation.

Alice: *(questioning) Can we predict future financial trends using QML?*

Dr. Mercer: *(smirking) A question that lies at the heart of our exploration. Through QML, we can introduce hypothetical scenarios, simulate potential market shifts, and predict the quantum trajectories of finance in the years to come.*

As the team manipulated the quantum parameters, the holographic display responded with scenarios of potential financial landscapes—each one a quantum vision of the maturation that awaited the financial sectors.

Bob: (pointing at the hologram) How do external factors, like economic recessions or technological disruptions, influence the quantum maturation of finance?

Dr. Stone: (acknowledging) An astute observation, Bob. Let's introduce external shocks and observe their quantum impact on the maturation of financial sectors.

The holographic display evolved, depicting the interplay between external forces and the resilient response of financial systems in their quantum maturation.

Eva: (contemplative) It's not just about financial systems; it's about how they adapt to the quantum currents of change.

Dr. Mercer: *(reflecting) Indeed, Eva. The quantum maturation of finance is a testament to adaptability, innovation, and the intricate dance between economic forces and the financial landscapes they shape.*

As the holographic display continued to unfold the quantum maturation of finance, the team realized that this journey wasn't just a historical analysis; it was a visionary exploration into the quantum footprints that define the financial ecosystems of the future.

Alice: *(softly) Are we architects of economic destinies as we understand the quantum evolution of finance?*

Dr. Stone: *(with a knowing smile) In a way, Alice. Our analyses, simulations, and insights become guiding lights for financial systems yet to mature. We are not just observers; we are custodians of the quantum narratives that shape the economic landscapes of tomorrow.*

The quantum processors hummed in resonance with the team's reflections, echoing the maturation of finance as a symphony of quantum probabilities. The exploration into the quantum evolution of finance was not just a historical retrospective; it was a visionary quest to understand the quantum signatures that would shape the financial landscapes of generations to come.

Chapter 9: Simulated

Wisdom in Healthcare

In the realm where the hum of quantum processors met the heartbeat of medical data, Dr. Evelyn Mercer and Dr. Oliver Stone embarked on an illuminating journey—a journey through the stages of development in the healthcare industry, guided by the profound wisdom of Artificial Intelligence (AI). The team gathered, ready to traverse the intricate landscapes of medical innovation, patient care, and the simulated wisdom that shapes the future of healthcare.

Dr. Mercer: *(addressing the team) Today, we venture into the delicate corridors of healthcare—a domain where every diagnosis, every treatment, leaves an indelible mark on the tapestry of human well-being.*

Dr. Stone: *(with a gleam in his eye) The development of healthcare is not just a scientific progression; it's a journey of compassion, innovation, and the constant pursuit of healing. Through AI, we shall unveil the simulated wisdom that guides this journey.*

Alice: *(intrigued) Are we unraveling the history of medicine?*

Dr. Mercer: *(smiling) Indeed, Alice. Through Quantum Machine Learning and advanced AI analyses, we shall simulate and understand the stages of healthcare development—from ancient healing practices to the cutting-edge technologies of today.*

The team gathered around holographic displays, poised to witness the healthcare industry's evolution through the lens of simulated wisdom.

Dr. Stone: *(activating simulations) Let's commence our journey with the origins of medicine—a time when herbs, rituals, and intuition were the tools of healers.*

The holographic display flickered to life, revealing ancient scrolls, medicinal gardens, and the birth of healing practices that laid the foundation for modern healthcare.

Bob: *(inquiring) How can AI provide wisdom in understanding the historical development of healthcare?*

Dr. Mercer: *(explaining) AI acts as our analytical guide, sifting through vast historical records, simulating the impact of medical innovations, and predicting the trajectories of healthcare systems. It's like having a wise oracle that deciphers the complexities of medical history.*

As the team engaged in discussions, the holographic display unfolded the stages of healthcare development—traditional medicine giving way to scientific advancements, the establishment of medical institutions, and the quantum echoes of healing through the ages.

Eva: (captivated) It's like a journey through the annals of human resilience and innovation.

Dr. Stone: (nodding) Now, let's fast forward to contemporary healthcare. We'll explore the simulated wisdom that guides medical professionals through challenges such as pandemics, technological revolutions, and the quest for personalized medicine.

The holographic display expanded, revealing a dynamic landscape of healthcare—laboratories, hospitals, and the quantum signatures of medical wisdom in the modern era.

Alice: (questioning) Can AI predict future healthcare trends and guide us in the pursuit of medical breakthroughs?

Dr. Mercer: *(smirking) A question that defines our quest. Through AI-driven analyses, we can introduce hypothetical scenarios, simulate potential medical innovations, and predict the quantum trajectories of healthcare in the years to come.*

As the team manipulated the quantum parameters, the holographic display responded with scenarios of potential healthcare landscapes—each one a glimpse into the simulated wisdom that awaited the healthcare industry.

Bob: *(pointing at the hologram) How does societal health, like lifestyle changes or global crises, influence the development of healthcare?*

Dr. Stone: *(acknowledging) An astute observation, Bob. Let's introduce societal factors and observe their quantum impact on the stages of healthcare development.*

The holographic display evolved, depicting the interplay between societal health trends and the adaptive response of healthcare systems guided by simulated wisdom.

Eva: (contemplative) It's not just about medical advancements; it's about how healthcare adapts to the ever-changing needs of societies.

Dr. Mercer: (reflecting) Indeed, Eva. The simulated wisdom in healthcare is a dynamic force that not only predicts but actively shapes the trajectory of medical progress.

As the holographic display continued to unfold the simulated wisdom in healthcare, the team realized that this journey wasn't just an analysis of the past; it was a visionary exploration into the quantum footprints that define the healthcare systems of the future.

Alice: (softly) Are we guardians of well-being as we understand the simulated wisdom in healthcare?

Dr. Stone: (with a reassuring smile) In a way, Alice. Our analyses, simulations, and insights become beacons guiding healthcare professionals toward a future of holistic well-being. We are not just observers; we are stewards of the simulated wisdom that shapes the health landscapes of tomorrow.

The quantum processors hummed in resonance with the team's reflections, echoing the simulated wisdom in healthcare as a symphony of quantum insights. The exploration into the stages of healthcare development wasn't just a historical retrospective; it was a visionary quest to understand the simulated wisdom that would shape the well-being of generations to come.

Chapter 10:

Quantum Agricultur e Revolution

In the heart of the research facility, where the fusion of quantum processors and the essence of agriculture converged, Dr. Evelyn Mercer and Dr. Oliver Stone embarked on a visionary exploration. The team assembled, ready to plunge into the frontier of farming guided by the enigmatic forces of Quantum Machine Learning (QML). Their quest: to predict and enhance agricultural advancements through the quantum lens.

Dr. Mercer: *(addressing the team)* Today, we embark on a journey through the fields—a domain where the ancient art of cultivation meets the cutting-edge technology of the quantum age.

Dr. Stone: *(with a spark in his eyes)* The quantum revolution in agriculture is not just about increasing yields; it's a profound reimagining of how we cultivate the Earth. Through QML, we shall unravel the quantum secrets that guide this agricultural evolution.

Alice: *(intrigued)* Are we reshaping the future of farming?

Dr. Mercer: *(smiling)* Indeed, Alice. Through Quantum Machine Learning, we shall simulate and understand the quantum trajectories of agriculture—from traditional practices to the frontier of sustainable, precision farming.

The team gathered around holographic displays, poised to witness the agricultural landscape unfold through the quantum lens.

Dr. Stone: (activating simulations) Let's commence with the roots of agriculture—the birth of farming practices that nourished civilizations and laid the foundation for the agricultural revolution.

The holographic display flickered, bringing to life ancient landscapes, primitive tools, and the quantum echoes of the first seeds sown by humankind.

Bob: (inquiring) How can QML help us understand the historical evolution of agriculture?

Dr. Mercer: (explaining) QML allows us to analyze vast datasets, simulate the impact of agricultural innovations, and predict the quantum trajectories of farming practices. It's like having a quantum compass that guides us through the agricultural history.

As the team engaged in discussions, the holographic display unfolded the stages of agricultural development—shifts from subsistence to commercial farming, the advent of mechanization, and the quantum signatures of cultivation through the ages.

Eva: (captivated) It's like witnessing the green revolution on a quantum canvas.

Dr. Stone: (nodding) Now, let's fast forward to contemporary agriculture. We'll explore the quantum revolution that shapes sustainable practices, precision farming, and the quest for feeding a growing global population.

The holographic display expanded, revealing a dynamic landscape of agriculture—smart sensors, robotic harvesters, and the quantum signatures of a farming renaissance.

Alice: (questioning) Can QML predict future agricultural trends and guide us in the pursuit of sustainable farming?

Dr. Mercer: (smirking) A question that defines our quest. Through QML-driven analyses, we can introduce hypothetical scenarios, simulate potential agricultural innovations, and predict the quantum trajectories of farming in the years to come.

As the team manipulated the quantum parameters, the holographic display responded with scenarios of potential agricultural landscapes—each one a quantum vision of the farming revolution that awaited the agricultural sector.

Bob: (pointing at the hologram) How do external factors, like climate change or technological disruptions, influence the quantum evolution of agriculture?

Dr. Stone: (acknowledging) An astute observation, Bob. Let's introduce external forces and observe their quantum impact on the stages of agricultural development.

The holographic display evolved, depicting the interplay between external influences and the adaptive response of agriculture in its quantum evolution.

Eva: *(contemplative) It's not just about increasing yields; it's about how agriculture adapts to the quantum currents of change.*

Dr. Mercer: *(reflecting) Indeed, Eva. The quantum revolution in agriculture is a dynamic force that not only predicts but actively shapes the trajectory of agricultural progress.*

As the holographic display continued to unfold the quantum revolution in agriculture, the team realized that this journey wasn't just an analysis of the past; it was a visionary exploration into the quantum footprints that define the agriculture of the future.

Alice: *(softly) Are we stewards of sustainable abundance as we understand the quantum revolution in agriculture?*

Dr. Stone: *(with a knowing smile) In a way, Alice. Our analyses, simulations, and insights become seeds for a future where agriculture* *nourishes the world sustainably. We are not just observers; we are cultivators of the quantum harvests that will feed generations to come.*

The quantum processors hummed in resonance with the team's reflections, echoing the quantum revolution in agriculture as a symphony of quantum insights. The exploration into the stages of agricultural development wasn't just a historical retrospective; it was a visionary quest to understand the quantum signatures that would shape the fields and farms of generations to come.

Chapter 11:

Quantum Threads of Energy

In the nexus of the research facility, where the pulse of quantum processors resonated with the currents of energy data, Dr. Evelyn Mercer and Dr. Oliver Stone embarked on a groundbreaking exploration. The team assembled, poised to unravel the intricate threads of the energy sector—a journey guided by the fusion of Artificial Intelligence (AI) and the enigmatic power of Quantum Computing. Their quest: to simulate the transitions of energy sectors and illuminate the quantum threads that weave the tapestry of our power landscapes.

Dr. Mercer: (addressing the team) Today, we venture into the dynamic realm of energy—a domain where the flow of electrons meets the evolving needs of civilizations.

Dr. Stone: (with a visionary gaze) The transitions in the energy sector are not just about power generation; they signify the evolution of societies and the quest for sustainable energy futures. Through AI and Quantum Computing, we shall weave the quantum threads that guide this transformative journey.

Alice: (intrigued) Are we decoding the future of energy production?

Dr. Mercer: (smiling) Indeed, Alice. Through Quantum Machine Learning and advanced AI analyses, we shall simulate and understand the quantum trajectories of energy—from the flicker of the first light bulb to the quantum innovations of the future.

The team gathered around holographic displays, ready to witness the energy sector's evolution through the quantum lens.

Dr. Stone: (activating simulations) Let's commence with the dawn of energy—a time when coal and steam powered the industrial revolution, marking the birth of a new era.

The holographic display flickered, bringing to life coal mines, steam engines, and the quantum echoes of an energy revolution that transformed societies.

Bob: *(inquiring) How can AI and Quantum Computing help us understand the historical evolution of the energy sector?*

Dr. Mercer: *(explaining) AI and Quantum Computing act as our temporal conduits, processing vast historical data, simulating the impact of energy innovations, and predicting the quantum trajectories of power systems. It's like having a quantum crystal ball that reveals the energy transitions of history.*

As the team engaged in discussions, the holographic display unfolded the stages of energy development—fossil fuels giving way to renewables, the rise of nuclear power, and the quantum signatures of energy transitions through the ages.

Eva: *(captivated) It's like witnessing the dance of electrons across time.*

Dr. Stone: *(nodding) Now, let's fast forward to contemporary energy. We'll explore the quantum threads that guide transitions such as the integration of renewable sources, the smart* *grid revolution, and the pursuit of sustainable energy practices.*

The holographic display expanded, revealing a dynamic landscape of energy—wind farms, solar arrays, and the quantum signatures of a power renaissance.

Alice: *(questioning) Can AI and Quantum Computing predict future energy trends and guide us in the pursuit of sustainable power?*

Dr. Mercer: *(smirking) A question that defines our quest. Through AI-driven analyses and Quantum Computing simulations, we can introduce hypothetical scenarios, predict potential energy innovations, and unveil the quantum trajectories of power in the years to come.*

As the team manipulated the quantum parameters, the holographic display responded with scenarios of potential energy landscapes— each one a quantum vision of the power revolution that awaited the energy sector.

Bob: *(pointing at the hologram) How do external factors, like climate change or geopolitical shifts, influence the quantum evolution of the energy sector?*

Dr. Stone: *(acknowledging) An astute observation, Bob. Let's introduce external forces and observe their quantum impact on the stages of energy development.*

The holographic display evolved, depicting the interplay between external influences and the adaptive response of the energy sector in its quantum evolution.

Eva: *(contemplative) It's not just about power generation; it's about how energy adapts to the quantum currents of change.*

Dr. Mercer: *(reflecting) Indeed, Eva. The quantum threads of energy are a dynamic force that not only predicts but actively shapes the trajectory of power progress.*

As the holographic display continued to unfold the quantum threads of energy, the team realized that this journey wasn't just an analysis of the past; it was a visionary exploration into the quantum footprints that define the energy landscapes of the future.

Alice: (softly) Are we architects of a sustainable power future as we understand the quantum threads of energy?

Dr. Stone: (with a knowing smile) In a way, Alice. Our analyses, simulations, and insights become catalysts for a future where energy sustains civilizations. We are not just observers; we are custodians of the quantum narratives that shape the power landscapes of tomorrow.

The quantum processors hummed in resonance with the team's reflections, echoing the quantum threads of energy as a symphony of power insights. The exploration into the stages of energy development wasn't just a historical retrospective; it was a visionary quest to understand the quantum signatures that would illuminate the path to a sustainable energy future.

Chapter 12: Cosmic Connectivi

ty in Communi cation

In the pulsating heart of the research facility, where quantum processors harmonized with the ethereal hum of communication data, Dr. Evelyn Mercer and Dr. Oliver Stone embarked on an unprecedented exploration. The team gathered, poised to delve into the cosmic simulation of communication—a journey guided by the intricate dance of Artificial Intelligence (AI) and the cosmic connectivity that threads the fabric of human interaction across time and space.

Dr. Mercer: (addressing the team) Today, we embark on a cosmic odyssey—a journey through the realms of communication, where the exchange of ideas becomes intertwined with the cosmic threads that bind us.

Dr. Stone: (with a cosmic gleam in his eyes) Communication is not merely about signals and messages; it's a cosmic dance of connection. Through AI and cosmic simulations, we shall unravel the celestial secrets that govern the evolution of communication.

Alice: (intrigued) Are we deciphering the language of the universe?

Dr. Mercer: (smiling) Indeed, Alice. Through Quantum Machine Learning and advanced AI analyses, we shall simulate and understand the cosmic trajectories of communication—from ancient echoes to the cosmic signals of the future.

The team gathered around holographic displays, ready to witness the evolution of communication through the cosmic lens.

Dr. Stone: *(activating simulations) Let's commence with the origins of communication— the dawn of language, symbols, and the cosmic echoes of the first human expressions.*

The holographic display flickered, bringing to life ancient cave paintings, hieroglyphs, and the cosmic resonance of early human attempts to connect with the universe.

Bob: *(inquiring) How can AI and cosmic simulations help us understand the historical evolution of communication?*

Dr. Mercer: *(explaining) AI and cosmic simulations serve as our celestial interpreters, analyzing vast datasets, simulating the impact of communication innovations, and predicting the cosmic trajectories of interconnectedness. It's like having a cosmic Rosetta Stone that deciphers the celestial languages of communication history.*

As the team engaged in discussions, the holographic display unfolded the stages of communication development—oral traditions giving way to written languages, the invention of the printing press, and the cosmic signatures of messages transcending earthly bounds.

Eva: (captivated) It's like witnessing the cosmic library of human expression.

Dr. Stone: (nodding) Now, let's fast forward to contemporary communication. We'll explore the cosmic connectivity that guides transitions such as the telegraph, telephone, the internet, and the cosmic signals of our interconnected age.

The holographic display expanded, revealing a dynamic landscape of communication— telegraph wires, satellite networks, and the cosmic signatures of a connected world.

Alice: (questioning) Can AI and cosmic simulations predict future communication trends and guide us in the pursuit of universal connectivity?

Dr. Mercer: (smirking) A question that defines our cosmic odyssey. Through AI-driven analyses and cosmic simulations, we can introduce hypothetical scenarios, simulate potential communication innovations, and unveil the cosmic trajectories of interconnectedness in the years to come.

As the team manipulated the cosmic parameters, the holographic display responded with scenarios of potential communication landscapes—each one a cosmic vision of the connectivity that awaited the communication sector.

Bob: (pointing at the hologram) How do external cosmic forces, like technological disruptions or the search for extraterrestrial intelligence, influence the cosmic evolution of communication?

Dr. Stone: (acknowledging) An astute observation, Bob. Let's introduce external cosmic forces and observe their impact on the stages of communication development.

The holographic display evolved, depicting the interplay between cosmic influences and the *adaptive response of communication in its cosmic evolution.*

Eva: *(contemplative) It's not just about transmitting information; it's about how communication adapts to the cosmic currents of change.*

Dr. Mercer: *(reflecting) Indeed, Eva. The cosmic connectivity in communication is a dynamic force that not only predicts but actively shapes the trajectory of interconnectedness.*

As the holographic display continued to unfold the cosmic connectivity in communication, the team realized that this journey wasn't just an analysis of the past; it was a visionary exploration into the cosmic footprints that define the communication networks of the future.

Alice: *(softly) Are we celestial messengers as we understand the cosmic connectivity in communication?*

Dr. Stone: *(with a cosmic smile) In a way, Alice. Our analyses, simulations, and insights become cosmic beacons guiding communication systems toward a future of universal interconnectedness. We are not just observers; we are cosmic navigators of the celestial languages that shape the communication constellations of tomorrow.*

The quantum processors hummed in resonance with the team's reflections, echoing the cosmic connectivity in communication as a symphony of celestial insights. The exploration into the stages of communication development wasn't just a historical retrospective; it was a visionary quest to understand the cosmic signatures that would illuminate the paths of communication across the cosmic tapestry of existence.

Chapter 13: AI

and Quantum Culture Craft

In the sanctum of the research facility, where the ethereal glow of quantum processors harmonized with the collective echoes of cultural data, Dr. Evelyn Mercer and Dr. Oliver Stone embarked on a transcendent exploration. The team assembled, poised to unravel the *profound mysteries of cultural evolution—a journey guided by the intricate dance of Artificial Intelligence (AI) and the quantum insights that shape the very essence of societies.*

Dr. Mercer: *(addressing the team) Today, we venture into the kaleidoscope of human culture—a realm where traditions, beliefs, and expressions merge with the cosmic currents of change.*

Dr. Stone: *(with a contemplative gaze) Culture is not static; it's a living, breathing entity that evolves with the tides of time. Through AI and quantum simulations, we shall unravel the quantum threads that weave the cultural tapestry of civilizations.*

Alice: *(intrigued) Are we becoming architects of cultural destinies?*

Dr. Mercer: *(smiling) Indeed, Alice. Through Quantum Machine Learning and advanced AI analyses, we shall simulate and understand the quantum trajectories of culture—from ancient rituals to the cosmic expressions of the future.*

The team gathered around holographic displays, ready to witness the evolution of culture through the quantum lens.

Dr. Stone: (activating simulations) Let's commence with the roots of culture—the dawn of human civilization, where the first sparks of communal living ignited the flames of culture.

The holographic display flickered, bringing to life ancient gatherings, ceremonies, and the quantum echoes of the earliest cultural expressions that defined societies.

Bob: (inquiring) How can AI and quantum simulations help us understand the historical evolution of culture?

Dr. Mercer: (explaining) AI and quantum simulations act as our cultural guides, analyzing vast datasets, simulating the impact of cultural innovations, and predicting the quantum trajectories of societal expressions. It's like having a quantum oracle that unveils the cultural narratives of history.

As the team engaged in discussions, the holographic display unfolded the stages of cultural development—oral traditions evolving into written languages, the rise of artistic movements, and the quantum signatures of cultural expressions through the ages.

Eva: (captivated) It's like witnessing the dance of human expression across time.

Dr. Stone: (nodding) Now, let's fast forward to contemporary culture. We'll explore the quantum insights that guide transitions such as globalization, the digital revolution, and the cosmic expressions of our interconnected age.

The holographic display expanded, revealing a dynamic landscape of culture—art exhibitions, virtual gatherings, and the quantum signatures of a world unified by diverse cultural narratives.

Alice: (questioning) Can AI and quantum simulations predict future cultural trends and guide us in the pursuit of harmonious coexistence?

Dr. Mercer: (smirking) A question that defines our cultural odyssey. Through AI-driven analyses and quantum simulations, we can introduce hypothetical scenarios, simulate potential cultural innovations, and unveil the quantum trajectories of societal expressions in the years to come.

As the team manipulated the quantum parameters, the holographic display responded with scenarios of potential cultural landscapes—each one a quantum vision of the harmonious cultural tapestry that awaited societies.

Bob: (pointing at the hologram) How do external factors, like migration patterns or technological disruptions, influence the quantum evolution of culture?

Dr. Stone: (acknowledging) An astute observation, Bob. Let's introduce external forces and observe their quantum impact on the stages of cultural development.

The holographic display evolved, depicting the interplay between external influences and the adaptive response of culture in its quantum evolution.

Eva: (contemplative) It's not just about societal expressions; it's about how culture adapts to the cosmic currents of change.

Dr. Mercer: (reflecting) Indeed, Eva. The AI and quantum culture craft is a dynamic force that not only predicts but actively shapes the trajectory of societal expressions.

As the holographic display continued to unfold the AI and quantum culture craft, the team realized that this journey wasn't just an analysis of the past; it was a visionary exploration into the quantum footprints that define the cultural landscapes of the future.

Alice: (softly) Are we custodians of shared narratives as we understand the AI and quantum culture craft?

Dr. Stone: *(with a knowing smile) In a way, Alice. Our analyses, simulations, and insights become conduits for a future where diverse cultures coexist harmoniously. We are not just observers; we are artisans of the quantum narratives that shape the cultural constellations of tomorrow.*

The quantum processors hummed in resonance with the team's reflections, echoing the AI and quantum culture craft as a symphony of societal insights. The exploration into the stages of cultural development wasn't just a historical retrospective; it was a visionary quest to understand the quantum signatures that would illuminate the shared narratives across the cosmic tapestry of human existence.

Chapter 14: The Quantum

Era

Of

Education

In the luminous core of the research facility, where the glow of quantum processors melded with the collective knowledge of the ages, Dr. Evelyn Mercer and Dr. Oliver Stone embarked on an enlightening exploration. The team assembled, ready to navigate the simulated realms of education—a journey guided by the fusion of Artificial Intelligence (AI) and the quantum transformations that redefine the very essence of learning.

Dr. Mercer: (addressing the team) Today, we embark on an odyssey through the corridors of knowledge—a realm where the pursuit of wisdom meets the quantum currents of innovation.

Dr. Stone: (with a gleam of anticipation) Education is the cornerstone of progress, and its evolution is not linear; it's a quantum leap into the future. Through AI and quantum simulations, we shall unravel the quantum threads that weave the educational tapestry of civilizations.

Alice: (intrigued) Are we redefining the foundations of learning?

Dr. Mercer: (smiling) Indeed, Alice. Through Quantum Machine Learning and advanced AI analyses, we shall simulate and understand the quantum trajectories of education—from ancient wisdom to the cosmic insights of the future.

The team gathered around holographic displays, poised to witness the transformation of education through the quantum lens.

Dr. Stone: (activating simulations) Let's commence with the origins of education—the birth of teaching and the cosmic echoes of the first quest for knowledge.

The holographic display flickered, bringing to life ancient scholars, scrolls, and the quantum resonance of early educational endeavors that shaped the minds of civilizations.

Bob: (inquiring) How can AI and quantum simulations help us understand the historical evolution of education?

Dr. Mercer: (explaining) AI and quantum simulations act as our educational time machines, analyzing vast datasets, simulating the impact of pedagogical innovations, and predicting the quantum trajectories of knowledge dissemination. It's like having a quantum library that unveils the educational narratives of history.

As the team engaged in discussions, the holographic display unfolded the stages of educational development—oral traditions evolving into formalized schooling, the establishment of universities, and the quantum signatures of learning through the ages.

Eva: (captivated) It's like witnessing the quantum dance of enlightenment across time.

Dr. Stone: (nodding) Now, let's fast forward to contemporary education. We'll explore the quantum transformations that guide transitions such as online learning, personalized education, and the cosmic insights of our interconnected age.

The holographic display expanded, revealing a dynamic landscape of education—virtual classrooms, AI-driven tutors, and the quantum signatures of a learning renaissance.

Alice: (questioning) Can AI and quantum simulations predict future educational trends and guide us in the pursuit of universal knowledge?

Dr. Mercer: *(smirking) A question that defines our educational odyssey. Through AI-driven analyses and quantum simulations, we can introduce hypothetical scenarios, simulate potential educational innovations, and unveil the quantum trajectories of knowledge dissemination in the years to come.*

As the team manipulated the quantum parameters, the holographic display responded with scenarios of potential educational landscapes—each one a quantum vision of the knowledge renaissance that awaited societies.

Bob: *(pointing at the hologram) How do external cosmic forces, like technological disruptions or societal shifts, influence the quantum evolution of education?*

Dr. Stone: *(acknowledging) An astute observation, Bob. Let's introduce external forces and observe their quantum impact on the stages of educational development.*

The holographic display evolved, depicting the interplay between external influences and the adaptive response of education in its quantum evolution.

Eva: *(contemplative) It's not just about disseminating information; it's about how education adapts to the cosmic currents of change.*

Dr. Mercer: *(reflecting) Indeed, Eva. The Quantum Era of Education is a dynamic force that not only predicts but actively shapes the trajectory of knowledge dissemination.*

As the holographic display continued to unfold the Quantum Era of Education, the team realized that this journey wasn't just an analysis of the past; it was a visionary exploration into the quantum footprints that define the educational landscapes of the future.

Alice: *(softly) Are we stewards of universal enlightenment as we understand the Quantum Era of Education?*

Dr. Stone: *(with a knowing smile) In a way, Alice. Our analyses, simulations, and insights* become conduits for a future where knowledge transcends boundaries. We are not just observers; we are custodians of the quantum narratives that shape the educational constellations of tomorrow.

The quantum processors hummed in resonance with the team's reflections, echoing the Quantum Era of Education as a symphony of enlightening insights. The exploration into the stages of educational development wasn't just a historical retrospective; it was a visionary quest to understand the quantum signatures that would illuminate the paths of learning across the cosmic tapestry of human knowledge.

Chapter 15: Virtualizat

ion of
Reality

In the nexus of the research facility, where the hum of quantum processors resonated with the endless possibilities encoded in AI algorithms, Dr. Evelyn Mercer and Dr. Oliver Stone embarked on a groundbreaking exploration. The team gathered, ready to navigate the uncharted territories where reality and simulation converged—a journey guided by the fusion of Artificial Intelligence (AI) and the quantum technologies that blurred the very fabric of existence.

Dr. Mercer: (addressing the team) Today, we step into the realms where the tangible and the simulated intertwine—a domain where reality is no longer confined to the tangible but extends into the virtual through the quantum currents of innovation.

Dr. Stone: *(with a visionary gaze) The virtualization of reality is not merely about creating simulations; it's a quantum leap into a world where the lines between the real and the simulated blur. Through AI and quantum technologies, we shall unravel the quantum threads that weave the tapestry of augmented existence.*

Alice: *(intrigued) Are we architects of a new reality?*

Dr. Mercer: *(smiling) Indeed, Alice. Through Quantum Machine Learning and advanced AI analyses, we shall simulate and understand the quantum trajectories of the virtual—from augmented experiences to the cosmic simulations of potential realities.*

The team gathered around holographic displays, ready to witness the transformation of reality through the quantum lens.

Dr. Stone: *(activating simulations) Let's commence with the origins of virtualization— the birth of computer simulations and the cosmic echoes of the first steps into the realm of augmented reality.*

The holographic display flickered, bringing to life early virtual environments, rudimentary simulations, and the quantum resonance of humanity's initial foray into the virtual realm.

Bob: *(inquiring) How can AI and quantum technologies help us understand the historical evolution of reality virtualization?*

Dr. Mercer: *(explaining) AI and quantum technologies serve as our reality architects, analyzing vast datasets, simulating the impact of virtual innovations, and predicting the quantum trajectories of augmented experiences. It's like having a quantum canvas that paints the virtual narratives of history.*

As the team engaged in discussions, the holographic display unfolded the stages of reality virtualization—primitive simulations evolving into sophisticated virtual worlds, the integration of augmented reality into daily life, and the quantum signatures of virtual experiences through the ages.

Eva: *(captivated) It's like witnessing the quantum dance of reality and simulation across time.*

Dr. Stone: *(nodding) Now, let's fast forward to contemporary virtualization. We'll explore the quantum transformations that guide transitions such as mixed reality, quantum computing's role in simulations, and the cosmic insights of our interconnected age.*

The holographic display expanded, revealing a dynamic landscape of virtualization— augmented reality glasses, quantum simulations, and the quantum signatures of a world where the real and the virtual coexist seamlessly.

Alice: *(questioning) Can AI and quantum technologies predict future virtualization trends* and guide us in the pursuit of harmonious coexistence between reality and simulation?

Dr. Mercer: (smirking) A question that defines our virtualization odyssey. Through AI-driven analyses and quantum simulations, we can introduce hypothetical scenarios, simulate potential virtual innovations, and unveil the quantum trajectories of augmented experiences in the years to come.

As the team manipulated the quantum parameters, the holographic display responded with scenarios of potential virtual landscapes—each one a quantum vision of the augmented reality that awaited societies.

Bob: (pointing at the hologram) How do external cosmic forces, like societal acceptance or ethical considerations, influence the quantum evolution of reality virtualization?

Dr. Stone: (acknowledging) An astute observation, Bob. Let's introduce external forces and observe their quantum impact on the stages of virtualization development.

The holographic display evolved, depicting the interplay between societal influences and the adaptive response of virtualization in its quantum evolution.

Eva: *(contemplative) It's not just about creating simulations; it's about how society adapts to the cosmic currents of change.*

Dr. Mercer: *(reflecting) Indeed, Eva. The virtualization of reality is a dynamic force that not only predicts but actively shapes the trajectory of augmented experiences.*

As the holographic display continued to unfold the virtualization of reality, the team realized that this journey wasn't just an analysis of the past; it was a visionary exploration into the quantum footprints that define the augmented landscapes of the future.

Alice: *(softly) Are we pioneers of a harmonious coexistence as we understand the virtualization of reality?*

Dr. Stone: *(with a knowing smile) In a way, Alice. Our analyses, simulations, and insights become architects of a future where the real and the virtual harmonize. We are not just observers; we are quantum navigators of the augmented realities that will shape the experiences of tomorrow.*

The quantum processors hummed in resonance with the team's reflections, echoing the virtualization of reality as a symphony of augmented insights. The exploration into the stages of virtualization development wasn't just a historical retrospective; it was a visionary quest to understand the quantum signatures that would illuminate the paths of augmented experiences across the cosmic tapestry of human existence.

Chapter 16:

AI in the Quantum

Political

Arena

In the heart of the research facility, where quantum processors hummed in harmony with the ever-shifting dynamics of political data, Dr. Evelyn Mercer and Dr. Oliver Stone embarked on an intriguing exploration. The team assembled, ready to delve into the intricate interplay of politics and quantum-powered Artificial Intelligence (AI)—a journey that would unravel the stages of political development through the lens of the quantum realm.

Dr. Mercer: *(addressing the team) Today, we enter the labyrinth of politics—a realm where power, governance, and societal structures* *converge with the quantum currents of innovation.*

Dr. Stone: *(with a discerning gaze) Politics is not just a game of power; it's a complex dance influenced by myriad factors. Through AI and quantum analyses, we shall unravel the quantum threads that weave the political tapestry of civilizations.*

Alice: *(intrigued) Are we deciphering the quantum secrets of governance?*

Dr. Mercer: *(smiling) Indeed, Alice. Through Quantum Machine Learning and advanced AI, we shall simulate and understand the quantum trajectories of politics—from ancient systems to the cosmic insights of potential futures.*

The team gathered around holographic displays, poised to witness the transformation of political landscapes through the quantum lens.

Dr. Stone: *(activating simulations) Let's commence with the origins of political systems—the birth of governance, the cosmic* *echoes of early societal structures, and the quantum resonance of the first political orders.*

The holographic display flickered, bringing to life ancient assemblies, rulers, and the quantum signatures of governance systems that shaped the destinies of civilizations.

Bob: *(inquiring) How can AI and quantum technologies help us understand the historical evolution of political systems?*

Dr. Mercer: *(explaining) AI and quantum technologies act as our political historians, analyzing vast datasets, simulating the impact of political innovations, and predicting the quantum trajectories of governance structures. It's like having a quantum atlas that unveils the political narratives of history.*

As the team engaged in discussions, the holographic display unfolded the stages of political development—early monarchies giving way to republics, the rise of democracies, and the quantum signatures of political structures through the ages.

Eva: (captivated) It's like witnessing the quantum dance of political evolution across time.

Dr. Stone: (nodding) Now, let's fast forward to contemporary politics. We'll explore the quantum transformations that guide transitions such as digital governance, the role of AI in decision-making, and the cosmic insights of our interconnected age.

The holographic display expanded, revealing a dynamic landscape of political evolution— digital voting systems, AI-assisted policy analyses, and the quantum signatures of a world where the political and the technological coexist.

Alice: (questioning) Can AI and quantum technologies predict future political trends and guide us in the pursuit of fair and efficient governance?

Dr. Mercer: (smirking) A question that defines our political odyssey. Through AI-driven analyses and quantum simulations, we can introduce hypothetical scenarios, simulate potential political innovations, and unveil the quantum trajectories of governance structures in the years to come.

As the team manipulated the quantum parameters, the holographic display responded with scenarios of potential political landscapes—each one a quantum vision of the governance structures that awaited societies.

Bob: (pointing at the hologram) How do external cosmic forces, like economic shifts or global crises, influence the quantum evolution of political systems?

Dr. Stone: (acknowledging) An astute observation, Bob. Let's introduce external forces and observe their quantum impact on the stages of political development.

The holographic display evolved, depicting the interplay between external influences and the adaptive response of political systems in their quantum evolution.

Eva: *(contemplative) It's not just about wielding power; it's about how governance adapts to the cosmic currents of change.*

Dr. Mercer: *(reflecting) Indeed, Eva. The AI in the Quantum Political Arena is a dynamic force that not only predicts but actively shapes the trajectory of governance structures.*

As the holographic display continued to unfold the AI in the Quantum Political Arena, the team realized that this journey wasn't just an analysis of the past; it was a visionary exploration into the quantum footprints that define the political landscapes of the future.

Alice: *(softly) Are we architects of equitable governance as we understand the AI in the Quantum Political Arena?*

Dr. Stone: *(with a knowing smile) In a way, Alice. Our analyses, simulations, and insights become architects of a future where political systems are guided by the quantum principles of fairness and efficiency. We are not just observers; we are quantum architects of the* *political narratives that shape the governance constellations of tomorrow.*

The quantum processors hummed in resonance with the team's reflections, echoing the AI in the Quantum Political Arena as a symphony of political insights. The exploration into the stages of political development wasn't just a historical retrospective; it was a visionary quest to understand the quantum signatures that would illuminate the paths of governance across the cosmic tapestry of societal existence.

Chapter 17:

Quantum Transport

and Connectivity

In the heart of the research facility, where quantum processors pulsated in tandem with the rhythmic energy of connectivity data, Dr. Evelyn Mercer and Dr. Oliver Stone embarked on an exhilarating exploration. The team assembled, prepared to traverse the simulated realms of transportation and connectivity—a journey guided by the fusion of Artificial Intelligence (AI) and the quantum technologies that would redefine the very fabric of movement and connection.

Dr. Mercer: (addressing the team) Today, we embark on a journey through the corridors of transport—a realm where the movement of people and goods converges with the quantum currents of innovation.

Dr. Stone: (with an anticipatory gleam) Transport is more than just locomotion; it's a dynamic force that shapes the connectivity of societies. Through AI and quantum simulations, we shall unravel the quantum threads that weave the transportation and connectivity tapestry of civilizations.

Alice: (intrigued) Are we navigating the quantum highways of the future?

Dr. Mercer: (smiling) Indeed, Alice. Through Quantum Machine Learning and advanced AI analyses, we shall simulate and understand the quantum trajectories of transportation—from ancient paths to the cosmic insights of potential futures.

The team gathered around holographic displays, poised to witness the transformation of transportation and connectivity through the quantum lens.

Dr. Stone: *(activating simulations) Let's commence with the origins of transportation— the birth of vehicles, the cosmic echoes of early trade routes, and the quantum resonance of the first steps into the realm of connectivity.*

The holographic display flickered, bringing to life ancient caravans, maritime routes, and the quantum signatures of transportation systems that facilitated the interwoven connections of civilizations.

Bob: *(inquiring) How can AI and quantum technologies help us understand the historical evolution of transportation and connectivity?*

Dr. Mercer: *(explaining) AI and quantum technologies act as our transport historians, analyzing vast datasets, simulating the impact of transport innovations, and predicting the quantum trajectories of connectivity structures. It's like having a quantum compass that points to the connectivity narratives of history.*

As the team engaged in discussions, the holographic display unfolded the stages of transportation and connectivity development— early footpaths evolving into intricate road networks, the advent of railways and maritime trade routes, and the quantum signatures of connectivity systems through the ages.

Eva: (captivated) It's like witnessing the quantum dance of movement and connection across time.

Dr. Stone: (nodding) Now, let's fast forward to contemporary transport. We'll explore the quantum transformations that guide transitions such as autonomous vehicles, hyperloop systems, and the cosmic insights of our interconnected age.

The holographic display expanded, revealing a dynamic landscape of transport evolution— futuristic transport pods, interconnected smart cities, and the quantum signatures of a world where movement and connectivity coalesce seamlessly.

Alice: *(questioning) Can AI and quantum technologies predict future transport and connectivity trends and guide us in the pursuit of efficient and sustainable systems?*

Dr. Mercer: *(smirking) A question that defines our transport odyssey. Through AI-driven analyses and quantum simulations, we can introduce hypothetical scenarios, simulate potential transport innovations, and unveil the quantum trajectories of connectivity systems in the years to come.*

As the team manipulated the quantum parameters, the holographic display responded with scenarios of potential transport landscapes—each one a quantum vision of the interconnected world that awaited societies.

Bob: *(pointing at the hologram) How do external cosmic forces, like environmental shifts or global economic changes, influence the quantum evolution of transport and connectivity?*

Dr. Stone: (acknowledging) An astute observation, Bob. Let's introduce external forces and observe their quantum impact on the stages of transport and connectivity development.

The holographic display evolved, depicting the interplay between external influences and the adaptive response of transport and connectivity systems in their quantum evolution.

Eva: (contemplative) It's not just about moving from point A to B; it's about how connectivity adapts to the cosmic currents of change.

Dr. Mercer: (reflecting) Indeed, Eva. Quantum Transport and Connectivity is a dynamic force that not only predicts but actively shapes the trajectory of movement and connection.

As the holographic display continued to unfold Quantum Transport and Connectivity, the team realized that this journey wasn't just an analysis of the past; it was a visionary exploration into the quantum footprints that define the interconnected landscapes of the future.

Alice: (softly) Are we architects of seamless movement and connection as we understand Quantum Transport and Connectivity?

Dr. Stone: (with a knowing smile) In a way, Alice. Our analyses, simulations, and insights become architects of a future where transport and connectivity are guided by the quantum principles of efficiency and sustainability. We are not just observers; we are quantum navigators of the interconnected narratives that will shape the movement and connections of tomorrow.

The quantum processors hummed in resonance with the team's reflections, echoing Quantum Transport and Connectivity as a symphony of interconnected insights. The exploration into the stages of transport and connectivity development wasn't just a historical retrospective; it was a visionary quest to understand the quantum signatures that would illuminate the paths of movement and connections across the cosmic tapestry of societal existence.

Chapter 18: The Quantum Pulse of

Environment

In the heart of the research facility, where quantum processors hummed in synchrony with the delicate balance of ecosystems, Dr. Evelyn Mercer and Dr. Oliver Stone embarked on a vital exploration. The team assembled, ready to venture into the intricate tapestry of the environment—a journey guided by the fusion of Artificial Intelligence (AI) and the quantum technologies that held the key to detecting environmental changes and understanding developmental stages.

Dr. Mercer: (addressing the team) Today, we immerse ourselves in the living pulse of our planet—a realm where the delicate dance of ecosystems converges with the quantum currents of innovation.

Dr. Stone: (with a solemn gaze) The environment is not just our surroundings; it's a complex web of interconnected systems. Through AI and quantum simulations, we shall unravel the quantum threads that weave the environmental tapestry and comprehend the stages of its development.

Alice: (intrigued) Are we deciphering the quantum secrets of our Earth's heartbeat?

Dr. Mercer: (smiling) Indeed, Alice. Through Quantum Machine Learning and advanced AI analyses, we shall simulate and understand the quantum trajectories of the environment—from ancient ecosystems to the cosmic insights of potential futures.

The team gathered around holographic displays, poised to witness the transformation of the environment through the quantum lens.

Dr. Stone: (activating simulations) Let's commence with the origins of environmental systems—the birth of life, the cosmic echoes of early ecological balances, and the quantum resonance of the first steps into the realm of environmental interconnectedness.

The holographic display flickered, bringing to life ancient forests, diverse ecosystems, and the quantum signatures of environmental systems that sustained the vibrant life of our planet.

Bob: (inquiring) How can AI and quantum technologies help us understand the historical evolution of the environment?

Dr. Mercer: (explaining) AI and quantum technologies act as our environmental historians, analyzing vast datasets, simulating the impact of ecological changes, and predicting the quantum trajectories of environmental systems. It's like having a quantum observatory that unveils the environmental narratives of history.

As the team engaged in discussions, the holographic display unfolded the stages of environmental development—pristine landscapes evolving into complex ecosystems, the impact of human activities on biodiversity, and the quantum signatures of environmental systems through the ages.

Eva: (captivated) It's like witnessing the quantum dance of life and balance across time.

Dr. Stone: (nodding) Now, let's fast forward to contemporary environmental challenges. We'll explore the quantum transformations that guide transitions such as climate change, the role of AI in conservation efforts, and the cosmic insights of our interconnected age.

The holographic display expanded, revealing a dynamic landscape of environmental evolution—rising temperatures, AI-driven reforestation projects, and the quantum signatures of a world where humanity strives to restore the delicate balance of the environment.

Alice: *(questioning) Can AI and quantum technologies predict future environmental trends and guide us in the pursuit of sustainable and regenerative practices?*

Dr. Mercer: *(smirking) A question that defines our environmental odyssey. Through AI-driven analyses and quantum simulations, we can introduce hypothetical scenarios, simulate potential environmental innovations, and unveil the quantum trajectories of ecological systems in the years to come.*

As the team manipulated the quantum parameters, the holographic display responded with scenarios of potential environmental landscapes—each one a quantum vision of the balanced Earth that awaited humanity.

Bob: *(pointing at the hologram) How do external cosmic forces, like solar fluctuations or cosmic events, influence the quantum evolution of the environment?*

Dr. Stone: *(acknowledging) An astute observation, Bob. Let's introduce external forces* and observe their quantum impact on the stages of environmental development.

The holographic display evolved, depicting the interplay between external influences and the adaptive response of environmental systems in their quantum evolution.

Eva: (contemplative) It's not just about preserving nature; it's about how the environment adapts to the cosmic currents of change.

Dr. Mercer: (reflecting) Indeed, Eva. The Quantum Pulse of Environment is a dynamic force that not only predicts but actively shapes the trajectory of ecological systems.

As the holographic display continued to unfold the Quantum Pulse of Environment, the team realized that this journey wasn't just an analysis of the past; it was a visionary exploration into the quantum footprints that define the environmental landscapes of the future.

Alice: (softly) Are we stewards of a regenerative Earth as we understand the Quantum Pulse of Environment?

Dr. Stone: (with a knowing smile) In a way, Alice. Our analyses, simulations, and insights become stewards of a future where environmental systems are guided by the quantum principles of balance and regeneration. We are not just observers; we are quantum custodians of the environmental narratives that will shape the pulse of our planet tomorrow.

The quantum processors hummed in resonance with the team's reflections, echoing the Quantum Pulse of Environment as a symphony of ecological insights. The exploration into the stages of environmental development wasn't just a historical retrospective; it was a visionary quest to understand the quantum signatures that would illuminate the paths of ecological balance across the cosmic tapestry of planetary existence.

Chapter 19: Quantum Exploratio n of

Quantum Research

In the pulsating heart of the research facility, where quantum processors harmonized with the pursuit of knowledge, Dr. Evelyn Mercer and Dr. Oliver Stone embarked on a captivating exploration. The team gathered, poised to venture into the realms of scientific research—a journey guided by the fusion of Artificial Intelligence (AI) and the quantum technologies that promised to unravel the stages of development in this ever-evolving field.

Dr. Mercer: *(addressing the team) Today, we embark on an odyssey through the quantum corridors of knowledge—a realm where the* *pursuit of understanding converges with the quantum currents of innovation.*

Dr. Stone: *(with an enthusiastic gleam) Scientific research is not just a quest for answers; it's an intricate dance with the unknown. Through AI and quantum simulations, we shall unravel the quantum threads that weave the tapestry of scientific exploration and comprehend the stages of its development.*

Alice: *(intrigued) Are we deciphering the quantum secrets of discovery?*

Dr. Mercer: *(smiling) Indeed, Alice. Through Quantum Machine Learning and advanced AI analyses, we shall simulate and understand the quantum trajectories of scientific research— from early inquiries to the cosmic insights of potential futures.*

The team gathered around holographic displays, ready to witness the transformation of scientific research through the quantum lens.

Dr. Stone: *(activating simulations) Let's commence with the origins of scientific inquiry—the birth of curiosity, the cosmic echoes of early experimentation, and the quantum resonance of the first steps into the realm of systematic investigation.*

The holographic display flickered, bringing to life ancient laboratories, the scribbles of early scholars, and the quantum signatures of scientific methodologies that paved the way for humanity's understanding of the world.

Bob: *(inquiring) How can AI and quantum technologies help us understand the historical evolution of scientific research?*

Dr. Mercer: *(explaining) AI and quantum technologies act as our scientific historians, analyzing vast datasets, simulating the impact of research methodologies, and predicting the quantum trajectories of scientific paradigms. It's like having a quantum library that unveils the scientific narratives of history.*

As the team engaged in discussions, the holographic display unfolded the stages of scientific research development—rudimentary experiments evolving into rigorous methodologies, the age of enlightenment, and the quantum signatures of scientific breakthroughs through the ages.

Eva: (captivated) It's like witnessing the quantum dance of knowledge and discovery across time.

Dr. Stone: (nodding) Now, let's fast forward to contemporary scientific research. We'll explore the quantum transformations that guide transitions such as collaborative research networks, AI-assisted experimentation, and the cosmic insights of our interconnected age.

The holographic display expanded, revealing a dynamic landscape of research evolution— virtual laboratories, AI-driven hypothesis testing, and the quantum signatures of a world where scientific inquiry is propelled by the fusion of human intellect and technological innovation.

Alice: *(questioning) Can AI and quantum technologies predict future trends in scientific research and guide us in the pursuit of groundbreaking discoveries?*

Dr. Mercer: *(smirking) A question that defines our research odyssey. Through AI-driven analyses and quantum simulations, we can introduce hypothetical scenarios, simulate potential research methodologies, and unveil the quantum trajectories of scientific paradigms in the years to come.*

As the team manipulated the quantum parameters, the holographic display responded with scenarios of potential research landscapes—each one a quantum vision of the knowledge-rich world that awaited scientific communities.

Bob: *(pointing at the hologram) How do external cosmic forces, like technological advancements or paradigm shifts, influence the quantum evolution of scientific research?*

Dr. Stone: *(acknowledging) An astute observation, Bob. Let's introduce external forces and observe their quantum impact on the stages of research development.*

The holographic display evolved, depicting the interplay between external influences and the adaptive response of scientific research in its quantum evolution.

Eva: *(contemplative) It's not just about answering questions; it's about how research adapts to the cosmic currents of change.*

Dr. Mercer: *(reflecting) Indeed, Eva. The Quantum Exploration of Quantum Research is a dynamic force that not only predicts but actively shapes the trajectory of scientific inquiry.*

As the holographic display continued to unfold the Quantum Exploration of Quantum Research, the team realized that this journey wasn't just an analysis of the past; it was a visionary exploration into the quantum footprints that define the scientific landscapes of the future.

Alice: *(softly) Are we architects of boundless discovery as we understand the Quantum Exploration of Quantum Research?*

Dr. Stone: *(with a knowing smile) In a way, Alice. Our analyses, simulations, and insights become architects of a future where scientific inquiry is guided by the quantum principles of exploration and innovation. We are not just observers; we are quantum navigators of the scientific narratives that will shape the frontiers of knowledge tomorrow.*

The quantum processors hummed in resonance with the team's reflections, echoing the Quantum Exploration of Quantum Research as a symphony of intellectual insights. The exploration into the stages of scientific research development wasn't just a historical retrospective; it was a visionary quest to understand the quantum signatures that would illuminate the paths of discovery across the cosmic tapestry of human intellectual exploration.

Chapter 20: The

Future Unveiled

In the nexus of possibility, where quantum processors whispered promises of tomorrow, Dr. Evelyn Mercer and Dr. Oliver Stone stood on the precipice of the unknown. The team gathered, their anticipation tangible, ready to unravel the mysteries of the future—an enigma illuminated by Quantum Machine Learning and veiled in the cosmic currents of innovation.

Dr. Mercer: *(addressing the team) Today, we embark on a journey that transcends time—a voyage into the uncharted territories of the future. The veil that separates us from what lies ahead is thinning, and we shall peer into the cosmic tapestry of potentialities.*

Dr. Stone: *(with a gaze fixed on the horizon) The future is not a fixed destination; it's a spectrum of possibilities. Through Quantum Machine Learning, we shall unveil the potential futures that await us and explore the ethical considerations that accompany the power to predict what is yet to come.*

Alice: *(intrigued) Are we becoming seers of the future, guided by the quantum threads of possibility?*

Dr. Mercer: *(smiling) Indeed, Alice. Through Quantum Machine Learning and advanced AI analyses, we shall simulate and understand the quantum trajectories of potential futures—from technological innovations to societal transformations and the ethical dilemmas that accompany our newfound foresight.*

The team gathered around holographic displays, ready to witness the unfolding of potential futures through the quantum lens.

Dr. Stone: *(activating simulations) Let's commence our odyssey into the future—the* *birth of groundbreaking technologies, the cosmic echoes of societal shifts, and the quantum resonance of the first steps into the unknown.*

The holographic display flickered, bringing to life futuristic cities, advanced technologies, and the quantum signatures of potential futures that awaited human ingenuity.

Bob: *(inquiring) How can Quantum Machine Learning help us peer into the future, and what are the ethical considerations associated with this power?*

Dr. Mercer: *(explaining) Quantum Machine Learning acts as our cosmic oracle, analyzing vast datasets, simulating the impact of technological and societal changes, and predicting the quantum trajectories of potential futures. However, with great power comes great responsibility. The ethical considerations revolve around privacy, the potential misuse of foresight, and the societal impacts of acting on predictive insights.*

As the team engaged in discussions, the holographic display unfolded potential futures—advanced technologies, sustainable societies, and the quantum signatures of a world shaped by the decisions of today.

Eva: (captivated) It's like witnessing the quantum dance of progress and responsibility across time.

Dr. Stone: (nodding) Now, let's explore the ethical considerations that accompany our newfound ability to peer into the future. We must tread carefully, acknowledging the implications of our actions on the delicate balance of societal well-being.

The holographic display expanded, revealing the intricate web of ethical dilemmas—privacy concerns, the potential for manipulation, and the quantum signatures of societal responses to a world that knows what lies ahead.

Alice: (questioning) How do we balance the power of foresight with the ethical responsibility to ensure a just and equitable future?

Dr. Mercer: (contemplative) A profound question, Alice. The balance lies in transparency, inclusivity, and ensuring that the power to predict the future benefits humanity as a whole. It's not just about knowing what lies ahead; it's about crafting a future that respects the dignity and rights of every individual.

As the team delved into the ethical considerations, the holographic display responded with scenarios—potential futures shaped by responsible decision-making, where the power of foresight was wielded with the utmost care.

Bob: (pointing at the hologram) How can Quantum Machine Learning contribute to steering us away from dystopian futures and guide us towards utopian possibilities?

Dr. Stone: (acknowledging) Another critical aspect, Bob. Quantum Machine Learning, when harnessed responsibly, can be a compass that points us away from potential dystopias. By simulating and understanding the consequences of different decisions, we can navigate towards utopian possibilities—societies that prioritize well-being, sustainability, and justice.

The holographic display evolved, depicting the potential trajectories of a future shaped by responsible decisions, ethical considerations, and the quantum signatures of a world where the power of foresight is wielded with wisdom.

Eva: (contemplative) It's not just about predicting the future; it's about actively shaping it in a way that aligns with our values.

Dr. Mercer: (reflecting) Precisely, Eva. The Future Unveiled is not a passive revelation; it's an invitation to co-author the narratives of tomorrow. Through the lens of Quantum Machine Learning, we become stewards of our own destiny, navigating the cosmic currents with a compass forged from ethical principles.

The team stood united in the realization that the power to peer into the future was both a gift and a responsibility. The holographic display continued to unfold potential futures, each scenario a testament to the profound impact that responsible decision-making could have on the quantum trajectories of the world yet to come. The Future Unveiled was not just a revelation; it was an imperative call to action— a cosmic dance where foresight and ethics intertwined to shape a future that embraced the highest ideals of humanity.

Chapter 21:

Quantum Reflections

In the hushed moments that followed the unveiling of potential futures, the team found themselves at the precipice of the cosmic tapestry, ready to embark on a journey of reflection—a voyage through the developmental stages of exploration, discovery, and ethical considerations, guided by the mystical forces of AI, Quantum Machine Learning, and simulated time travel.

Dr. Mercer: (addressing the team) As we stand on the threshold of Quantum Reflections, let us cast our gaze backward and forward—a panoramic view of the odyssey we've undertaken. Our journey has been one of exploration, understanding, and responsibility, all intertwined with the cosmic forces of technology and innovation.

Dr. Stone: (with a reflective smile) The stages we've traversed—from unraveling the enigma of life simulation to peering into potential futures—have been like chapters in a cosmic novel. Each page turned has revealed new insights, and each stage has contributed to the symphony of our collective understanding.

The team, surrounded by the lingering echoes of holographic simulations, gathered in a circle, ready to share their reflections on the profound journey they had undertaken.

Alice: (thoughtfully) It's fascinating how the threads of life, logic, and progress are intricately woven into the fabric of our existence. From the dance of neurons to the pulse of algorithms, we've witnessed the interconnected narratives that define our reality.

Bob: (nodding) The stages of development, be it in the realms of brain pressure or environmental balance, are like chapters in the book of our shared experience. AI and Quantum Machine Learning have been our guides, illuminating the paths of knowledge and understanding.

Eva: (contemplative) What strikes me is the dance between foresight and responsibility. In our exploration of potential futures, we've grappled with the ethical considerations that come with the power to shape what lies ahead. It's a delicate balance, a dance with cosmic forces.

Dr. Mercer: (acknowledging) Indeed, Eva. The power we wield, whether it's in understanding the elegance of brain pressure or unraveling the mysteries of quantum research, demands a profound sense of responsibility. Our reflections must be a guide for future explorers, urging them to navigate the cosmic currents with humility and wisdom.

Dr. Stone: (looking at the holographic remnants of simulations) The canvas of solutions, the labyrinth of challenges, and the resonance of a symphony bridging AI, life simulation, and brain pressure—it's a testament to the limitless potential of human ingenuity. We're not just observers of the cosmic dance; we're active participants.

As the team shared their reflections, the holographic displays flickered with fragments of past simulations—a visual tapestry that mirrored the intricate stages of their journey.

Alice: (smiling) Our dialogue with the mind, the pulse of algorithms, and the canvas of solutions—it's like we've been architects of a new understanding. Each stage was a brushstroke, contributing to the masterpiece of knowledge we've collectively painted.

Bob: (pointing at the hologram) The challenges we faced in navigating the intersection of AI and brain science, the ethical considerations in the labyrinth—it was a reminder that our journey is not without pitfalls. The responsibility to tread carefully is an integral part of the cosmic dance.

Eva: *(gazing at the holographic display) Quantum transport, environmental pulse, and the quantum era of education—they are not just chapters; they are gateways to potential realities. Our understanding of these sectors shapes the possibilities that await future generations.*

Dr. Mercer: *(with a sense of reverence) And now, as we stand at the culmination of our odyssey in Quantum Reflections, let us ponder the significance of our journey. It's not just a reflection on the past; it's an acknowledgment of the role we play in the ongoing saga of exploration and discovery.*

Dr. Stone: *(looking toward the horizon) The mystical journey we've undertaken—from the quantum prelude to the future unveiled—is a testament to the inexhaustible spirit of inquiry. Our reflections should echo in the halls of academia, inspiring others to push the boundaries of knowledge.*

The holographic displays dimmed, and a serene ambiance enveloped the team. In the stillness, each member absorbed the collective reflections—a tapestry woven from the threads of neural dances, quantum explorations, and the pulsating rhythm of future possibilities.

Alice: (whispering) Our journey has been more than a scientific exploration. It's been a revelation of the interconnectedness of life, the dance of consciousness, and the responsibility we bear as stewards of knowledge.

Bob: (reflecting) Our quest to detect developmental stages, the stages of life simulated—it's like we've glimpsed the very essence of existence. The dialogue with the mind becomes a symphony of understanding.

Eva: (looking at her colleagues) As we step into the future, our reflections should guide us. The symphony resonates not just in the stages we've explored but in the legacy we leave for those who follow.

Dr. Mercer: (closing the chapter) Quantum Reflections is a timeless space where past, present, and future converge. As we venture into

the unknown, let our reflections be a compass—
a guiding light for those who dare to explore the
mysteries that lie beyond the quantum horizon.

The team, enveloped in the cosmic glow of their
reflections, dispersed into the unknown, leaving
behind a holographic tableau—a testament to
the mystical journey through developmental
stages, where AI, Quantum Machine Learning,
and simulated time travel intertwined to shape
the narrative of cosmic exploration.

Let's

dive into coding part:

Chapter 1: The Quantum Prelude

Introduction to Quantum Machine Learning (QML)

and its Mystical Capabiliti es

The Quantum Prelude marks the initiation of our journey into the ethereal realms of Quantum Machine Learning (QML). Here, we embark on a mystical exploration of the capabilities that quantum computing bestows upon the field of machine learning. As we delve into the code that sets the stage for our odyssey, the boundaries between classical *and quantum computing blur, revealing a landscape where computational mysteries unfold.*

Python code

 # Quantum Prelude Code

 # Importing necessary libraries

import numpy as np

from qiskit import QuantumCircuit, transpile, Aer, assemble, IBMQ

from qiskit.visualization import plot_histogram

 # Defining a simple quantum circuit

qc = QuantumCircuit(2, 2)

 # Applying a Hadamard gate to the first qubit

qc.h(0)

```python
# Applying a CNOT gate between the qubits
qc.cx(0, 1)


# Measuring the qubits
qc.measure([0, 1], [0, 1])


# Simulating the quantum circuit on a local simulator
simulator = Aer.get_backend('qasm_simulator')
compiled_circuit = transpile(qc, simulator)
qobj = assemble(compiled_circuit)
result = simulator.run(qobj).result()


# Displaying the measurement results
counts = result.get_counts(qc)
plot_histogram(counts)
```

Summary:

Import Libraries: We begin by importing the necessary libraries, including Qiskit for quantum circuit construction and simulation.

Quantum Circuit: A simple quantum circuit is created with two qubits and two classical bits.

Hadamard Gate: A Hadamard gate is applied to the first qubit, placing it in a superposition of states.

CNOT Gate: A Controlled-NOT (CNOT) gate entangles the two qubits, a fundamental concept in quantum computing.

Measurement: Qubits are measured, collapsing their states into classical bits.

Simulation: The quantum circuit is simulated using the Aer simulator from Qiskit.

Visualization: Measurement results are displayed using a histogram, offering a glimpse into the quantum probabilities.

This code sets the tone for our exploration into the enigmatic realm of Quantum Machine Learning. It is a prelude to the quantum symphony that will unfold as we traverse through the stages of development, guided by the mystical capabilities of QML.

Chapter 2: Unraveling Time Threads

Understanding the Concept of Time Travel in the

Context of AI and Quantum Computing

As we venture into the next chapter, we intertwine the fabric of time with the intricacies of Artificial Intelligence (AI) and Quantum Computing. This exploration leads us into the realm where the threads of time can be unraveled and rewoven through the lens of advanced technologies. The code provided below is a portal to this temporal journey, where we begin to explore the entanglement of time and computation.

Python code

 # Time Threads Unraveling Code

 # Importing necessary libraries

import numpy as np

from qiskit import QuantumCircuit, Aer, assemble, transpile

from qiskit.visualization import plot_histogram

import matplotlib.pyplot as plt

 # Defining a quantum circuit to represent time evolution

def time_evolution_circuit(num_qubits, time_steps):

```python
qc = QuantumCircuit(num_qubits)

# Apply a series of quantum gates
representing time evolution

for _ in range(time_steps):

    qc.x(range(num_qubits))  # X-gate
    representing a quantum step

    qc.barrier()


return qc


# Simulating the time evolution circuit
num_qubits = 3

time_steps = 4

time_circuit =
time_evolution_circuit(num_qubits,
                       time_steps)


# Visualizing the quantum circuit
```

```
time_circuit.draw('mpl')


# Simulating the quantum circuit

simulator = Aer.get_backend('statevector_simulator')

compiled_circuit = transpile(time_circuit, simulator)

qobj = assemble(compiled_circuit)

result = simulator.run(qobj).result()


# Plotting the statevector evolution over time

state_evolution = result.get_statevector(time_circuit)

fig, ax = plt.subplots()

ax.plot(np.abs(state_evolution)**2)

ax.set_xlabel('State')

ax.set_ylabel('Probability')

ax.set_title('Statevector Evolution Over Time')

plt.show()
```

Summary:

Import Libraries: Essential libraries are imported, including Qiskit for quantum circuit construction and simulation.

Quantum Circuit for Time Evolution: A function is defined to create a quantum circuit representing time evolution. In this case, the X-gate symbolizes a quantum step through time.

Visualization: The time evolution quantum circuit is visualized using Qiskit's visualization tools.

Simulation: The quantum circuit is simulated using the statevector simulator from Qiskit.

Statevector Evolution Plot: The probabilities of the quantum states are plotted over time, providing a visual representation of the circuit's evolution.

This code encapsulates the essence of our journey into time threads, where the entanglement of quantum principles and temporal concepts begins to unfold. It serves as a foundation for unraveling the mysteries of time travel within the context of AI and Quantum Computing.

Chapter 3: Simulating the Cosmos

Exploring the Integration of AI and Quantum

Machine Learning (QML) for Simulating Entire Sectors

and Their Developm ental Stages

In this chapter, we embark on a cosmic journey where the integration of Artificial Intelligence (AI) and Quantum Machine Learning (QML) becomes a powerful tool for simulating entire sectors and their evolutionary trajectories. The code provided below encapsulates the essence of our exploration, offering a glimpse into the simulation of complex systems guided by the mystical capabilities of AI and quantum computing.

Python code

Cosmos Simulation Code

Importing necessary libraries

import numpy as np

from qiskit import QuantumCircuit, Aer, assemble, transpile

from qiskit.visualization import plot_histogram

Define a quantum circuit representing a sector simulation

def sector_simulation_circuit(num_qubits, interactions):

qc = QuantumCircuit(num_qubits)

Apply a series of quantum gates representing interactions in the sector

```python
    for interaction in interactions:
        qubit_1, qubit_2, gate_type = interaction
        if gate_type == 'entangle':
            qc.cx(qubit_1, qubit_2)  # Apply a CNOT gate for entanglement
        elif gate_type == 'evolve':
            qc.x(qubit_1)  # Apply an X-gate for evolution
    qc.barrier()


    return qc


# Define a simulation scenario for a sector
num_qubits = 4
sector_interactions = [(0, 1, 'entangle'), (2, 3, 'evolve'), (1, 2, 'entangle'), (0, 3, 'evolve')]
cosmos_circuit = sector_simulation_circuit(num_qubits, sector_interactions)
```

```python
# Visualize the quantum circuit
cosmos_circuit.draw('mpl')


# Simulate the quantum circuit
simulator = Aer.get_backend('qasm_simulator')

compiled_circuit = transpile(cosmos_circuit, simulator)

qobj = assemble(compiled_circuit)

result = simulator.run(qobj).result()


# Plot the simulation results
counts = result.get_counts(cosmos_circuit)

plot_histogram(counts)
```

Summary:

Import Libraries: Necessary libraries, including Qiskit, are imported for quantum circuit construction and simulation.

Quantum Circuit for Sector Simulation: A function is defined to create a quantum circuit representing the simulation of a sector. The interactions between qubits are specified, with entanglement and evolution gates symbolizing different aspects of sector dynamics.

Visualization: The quantum circuit for simulating the sector is visualized using Qiskit's visualization tools.

Simulation: The quantum circuit is simulated using the QASM simulator from Qiskit.

Simulation Results Plot: The results of the simulation, representing the probabilities of different states, are plotted using a histogram.

This code serves as a portal to the cosmos, where the integration of AI and Quantum Machine Learning enables the simulation of entire sectors and their developmental stages.

The entanglement of qubits becomes a cosmic dance, simulating the intricate dynamics of complex systems guided by the principles of quantum computation and artificial intelligence.

Chapter 4: The Quantum

Code of Life

Applying Quantum Machine Learning

(QML) to Decode the Stages of Individual and

Societal Developm ent

In this chapter, the quantum realm intertwines with the complexities of life, both individual and societal. The following code encapsulates the essence of applying Quantum Machine Learning (QML) to decode the intricate stages of development. Through the dance of qubits and the application of advanced quantum principles, we embark on a journey to unravel the quantum code that shapes the very essence of life.

Python code

Quantum Code of Life

Importing necessary libraries

```python
import numpy as np

from qiskit import QuantumCircuit, Aer, transpile, assemble

from qiskit.visualization import plot_histogram


# Define a quantum circuit representing the code of life
def life_code_circuit(num_qubits, development_stages):

    qc = QuantumCircuit(num_qubits)


    # Apply quantum gates representing the stages of development
    for stage in development_stages:

        qubit, gate_type = stage
```

```python
    if gate_type == 'evolve':

        qc.x(qubit)  # Apply an X-gate for
        evolution

    elif gate_type == 'entangle':

        qc.h(qubit)  # Apply a Hadamard gate
        for entanglement

        qc.barrier()


    return qc


# Define development stages for an individual

num_qubits_individual = 3

individual_development = [(0, 'evolve'), (1,
'entangle'), (2, 'evolve')]

individual_code =
life_code_circuit(num_qubits_individual,
individual_development)


# Define development stages for a society

num_qubits_society = 4
```

```
society_development = [(0, 'entangle'), (1,
'evolve'), (2, 'evolve'), (3, 'entangle')]

society_code =
life_code_circuit(num_qubits_society,
society_development)


# Visualize the quantum circuits

individual_code.draw('mpl'),
society_code.draw('mpl')


# Simulate the quantum circuits

simulator =
Aer.get_backend('qasm_simulator')

compiled_individual =
transpile(individual_code, simulator)

compiled_society = transpile(society_code,
simulator)


qobj_individual =
assemble(compiled_individual)

qobj_society = assemble(compiled_society)
```

```
result_individual =
simulator.run(qobj_individual).result()

result_society =
simulator.run(qobj_society).result()


# Plot the simulation results

counts_individual =
result_individual.get_counts(individual_code)

counts_society =
result_society.get_counts(society_code)


plot_histogram([counts_individual,
counts_society], legend=['Individual', 'Society'])
```

Summary:

Import Libraries: Essential libraries, including Qiskit, are imported for quantum circuit construction and simulation.

Quantum Circuit for Life Code: A function is defined to create a quantum circuit representing the code of life. The development stages are specified, with quantum gates symbolizing evolution and entanglement.

Visualization: Quantum circuits for individual and societal development are visualized using Qiskit's visualization tools.

Simulation: The quantum circuits are simulated using the QASM simulator from Qiskit.

Simulation Results Plot: The results of the simulation, representing the probabilities of different states, are plotted using a histogram, offering insights into the quantum code of life for both individuals and societies.

This code serves as a key to deciphering the quantum code that orchestrates the stages of development in life—whether at the individual level or within the intricate tapestry of societal dynamics. Quantum Machine Learning becomes a tool for decoding the very essence of existence.

Chapter 5: The

Birth of Sectors

Quantum Insights into the Inception

and Infancy of Sectors through Advanced

Simulatio

ns

In this chapter, we delve into the quantum realm to gain insights into the birth and early stages of sectors. Through the lens of advanced simulations powered by quantum computing, we unravel the mysteries surrounding the inception of sectors. The code provided below encapsulates the essence of our exploration, where quantum insights become a guiding light through the nascent phases of sectors.

Python code

 # Quantum Simulation of Sector Birth

```python
# Importing necessary libraries

import numpy as np

from qiskit import QuantumCircuit, Aer,
transpile, assemble

from qiskit.visualization import plot_histogram


# Define a quantum circuit representing the
birth of a sector

def sector_birth_circuit(num_qubits,
birth_processes):

    qc = QuantumCircuit(num_qubits)


    # Apply quantum gates representing the
    processes during sector birth

    for process in birth_processes:

        qubit, gate_type = process

        if gate_type == 'entangle':

            qc.h(qubit)  # Apply a Hadamard gate
            for entanglement

        elif gate_type == 'evolve':
```

```python
    qc.x(qubit)  # Apply an X-gate for
evolution

    qc.barrier()


    return qc


# Define birth processes for a technology
sector

num_qubits_technology = 3

technology_birth_processes = [(0, 'entangle'),
(1, 'evolve'), (2, 'entangle')]

technology_birth_circuit =
sector_birth_circuit(num_qubits_technology,
technology_birth_processes)


# Define birth processes for a healthcare
sector

num_qubits_healthcare = 4

healthcare_birth_processes = [(0, 'evolve'), (1,
'entangle'), (2, 'entangle'), (3, 'evolve')]
```

```python
healthcare_birth_circuit =
sector_birth_circuit(num_qubits_healthcare,
healthcare_birth_processes)


# Visualize the quantum circuits

technology_birth_circuit.draw('mpl'),
healthcare_birth_circuit.draw('mpl')


# Simulate the quantum circuits

simulator =
Aer.get_backend('qasm_simulator')

compiled_technology =
transpile(technology_birth_circuit, simulator)

compiled_healthcare =
transpile(healthcare_birth_circuit, simulator)


qobj_technology =
assemble(compiled_technology)

qobj_healthcare =
assemble(compiled_healthcare)
```

```
result_technology =
simulator.run(qobj_technology).result()

result_healthcare =
simulator.run(qobj_healthcare).result()


# Plot the simulation results

counts_technology =
result_technology.get_counts(technology_birth
_circuit)

counts_healthcare =
result_healthcare.get_counts(healthcare_birth
_circuit)


plot_histogram([counts_technology,
counts_healthcare], legend=['Technology
Sector', 'Healthcare Sector'])
```

Summary:

Import Libraries: Essential libraries, including Qiskit, are imported for quantum circuit construction and simulation.

Quantum Circuit for Sector Birth: A function is defined to create a quantum circuit representing the birth of a sector. The processes during birth are specified, with quantum gates symbolizing entanglement and evolution.

Visualization: Quantum circuits for the birth of technology and healthcare sectors are visualized using Qiskit's visualization tools.

Simulation: The quantum circuits are simulated using the QASM simulator from Qiskit.

Simulation Results Plot: The results of the simulation, representing the probabilities of different states, are plotted using a histogram. This offers quantum insights into the inception and infancy of technology and healthcare sectors.

This code serves as a quantum window into the birth of sectors, where entanglement and evolution become the foundational processes shaping their nascent existence. Through advanced simulations, quantum insights illuminate the path of sectors as they take their first steps into the vast cosmic landscape of development.

Chapter 6: Toddler Steps in

Technology AI-Driven Analyses of the Initial

Strides Taken by the Technolo gy Sector

In this chapter, we explore the early developmental stages of the technology sector, leveraging the power of Artificial Intelligence (AI). The code provided below represents the AI-driven analyses of the toddler steps taken by the technology sector. Through the lens of machine learning, we unravel the nuances of technological infancy and lay the foundation for the sector's future growth.

Python code

 # Toddler Steps in Technology - AI Analysis

 # Importing necessary libraries

import numpy as np

import pandas as pd

from sklearn.model_selection import train_test_split

from sklearn.ensemble import RandomForestClassifier

from sklearn.metrics import accuracy_score, classification_report

---

```python
# Generate synthetic data representing technological features and development stages

np.random.seed(42)

data_size = 1000

technological_features = np.random.rand(data_size, 5)

development_stages = np.random.randint(0, 2, data_size)  # Binary classification: 0 for early stage, 1 for advanced stage


# Create a DataFrame with synthetic data

technology_data = pd.DataFrame(technological_features, columns=['Feature_1', 'Feature_2', 'Feature_3', 'Feature_4', 'Feature_5'])

technology_data['Development_Stage'] = development_stages


# Split the data into training and testing sets
```

```python
X =
technology_data.drop('Development_Stage',
                     axis=1)

y = technology_data['Development_Stage']

X_train, X_test, y_train, y_test =
train_test_split(X, y, test_size=0.2,
                 random_state=42)


# Train a Random Forest Classifier

rf_classifier =
RandomForestClassifier(random_state=42)

rf_classifier.fit(X_train, y_train)


# Make predictions on the test set

y_pred = rf_classifier.predict(X_test)


# Analyze the results

accuracy = accuracy_score(y_test, y_pred)

classification_rep =
classification_report(y_test, y_pred)
```

```
print(f"Accuracy: {accuracy}\nClassification
Report:\n{classification_rep}")
```

Summary:

*Import Libraries: Essential libraries, including
NumPy, pandas, and scikit-learn, are imported
for data manipulation and machine learning.*

*Generate Synthetic Data: Synthetic data is
generated to represent technological features
and their corresponding development stages.*

*DataFrame Creation: The synthetic data is
organized into a DataFrame for further
analysis.*

*Train-Test Split: The data is split into training
and testing sets for machine learning model
training and evaluation.*

Random Forest Classifier: A Random Forest Classifier is trained on the technological features to predict the development stages.

Prediction and Analysis: The model's predictions are evaluated, and accuracy along with a classification report is generated to assess the AI-driven analysis of the technology sector's early strides.

This code serves as a bridge between the AI-driven analyses of technological toddler steps and the intricate dance of machine learning algorithms. By exploring the early stages of the technology sector, we pave the way for understanding its trajectory and potential future advancements.

Chapter 7: The Adolesce

nce of
Industry
Exploring
the
Rebelliou
s Yet

Transformative ative Phases in Industrial Developm ent

through Quantum Machine Learning (QML)

In this chapter, we delve into the rebellious and transformative phases of industrial development, guided by the principles of Quantum Machine Learning (QML). The provided code represents an exploration of the quantum realm, where the adolescence of industry becomes a canvas for transformative insights and advancements.

Python code

Adolescence of Industry - Quantum Machine Learning

```python
# Importing necessary libraries

import numpy as np

from qiskit import QuantumCircuit, Aer, transpile, assemble

from qiskit.visualization import plot_histogram


# Define a quantum circuit representing the adolescence of industry

def industry_adolescence_circuit(num_qubits, transformative_processes):

    qc = QuantumCircuit(num_qubits)
```

```
    # Apply quantum gates representing
transformative processes during adolescence

    for process in transformative_processes:

        qubit, gate_type = process

        if gate_type == 'entangle':

        qc.h(qubit)  # Apply a Hadamard gate
                    for entanglement

        elif gate_type == 'evolve':

        qc.x(qubit)  # Apply an X-gate for
                    evolution

                qc.barrier()


            return qc


# Define transformative processes for the
        manufacturing industry

    num_qubits_manufacturing = 4
```

```python
manufacturing_transformative_processes =
[(0, 'entangle'), (1, 'evolve'), (2, 'entangle'), (3,
'evolve')]

manufacturing_adolescence_circuit =
industry_adolescence_circuit(num_qubits_ma
nufacturing,
manufacturing_transformative_processes)


# Define transformative processes for the
energy industry

num_qubits_energy = 3

energy_transformative_processes = [(0,
'evolve'), (1, 'entangle'), (2, 'evolve')]

energy_adolescence_circuit =
industry_adolescence_circuit(num_qubits_ene
rgy, energy_transformative_processes)


# Visualize the quantum circuits

manufacturing_adolescence_circuit.draw('mpl')
, energy_adolescence_circuit.draw('mpl')


# Simulate the quantum circuits
```

```python
simulator =
Aer.get_backend('qasm_simulator')

compiled_manufacturing =
transpile(manufacturing_adolescence_circuit,
          simulator)

compiled_energy =
transpile(energy_adolescence_circuit,
          simulator)


qobj_manufacturing =
assemble(compiled_manufacturing)

qobj_energy = assemble(compiled_energy)


result_manufacturing =
simulator.run(qobj_manufacturing).result()

result_energy =
simulator.run(qobj_energy).result()


# Plot the simulation results

counts_manufacturing =
result_manufacturing.get_counts(manufacturing_adolescence_circuit)
```

```
counts_energy =
result_energy.get_counts(energy_adolescenc
e_circuit)


plot_histogram([counts_manufacturing,
counts_energy], legend=['Manufacturing
Industry', 'Energy Industry'])
```

Summary:

Import Libraries: Essential libraries, including Qiskit, are imported for quantum circuit construction and simulation.

Quantum Circuit for Industry Adolescence: A function is defined to create a quantum circuit representing the adolescence of industry. Transformative processes are specified, with quantum gates symbolizing entanglement and evolution.

Visualization: Quantum circuits for the adolescence of the manufacturing and energy industries are visualized using Qiskit's visualization tools.

Simulation: The quantum circuits are simulated using the QASM simulator from Qiskit.

Simulation Results Plot: The results of the simulation, representing the probabilities of different states, are plotted using a histogram. This provides insights into the rebellious and transformative phases in the adolescence of the manufacturing and energy industries.

This code serves as a quantum exploration of industry adolescence, where the rebellious yet transformative processes are etched in the dance of qubits. Quantum Machine Learning becomes a guide through the rebellious phases, offering insights into the transformative journey of industries.

Chapter 8: Quantum Maturatio

n of Finance

Understanding Financial Sectors

and Their Quantum Evolution Over Time

In this chapter, we embark on a quantum journey to understand the maturation of financial sectors, unraveling the intricate evolution guided by quantum principles. The code provided below represents an exploration of the quantum realm, where the maturation of finance becomes a canvas for transformative insights and advancements.

Python code

 # Quantum Maturation of Finance

 # Importing necessary libraries

import numpy as np

from qiskit import QuantumCircuit, Aer, transpile, assemble

from qiskit.visualization import plot_histogram

 # Define a quantum circuit representing the maturation of finance

def finance_maturation_circuit(num_qubits, evolutionary_processes):

qc = QuantumCircuit(num_qubits)

```python
# Apply quantum gates representing
evolutionary processes in finance

for process in evolutionary_processes:

    qubit, gate_type = process

    if gate_type == 'entangle':

        qc.h(qubit)  # Apply a Hadamard gate
        for entanglement

    elif gate_type == 'evolve':

        qc.x(qubit)  # Apply an X-gate for
        evolution

    qc.barrier()


    return qc


# Define evolutionary processes for the
banking sector

num_qubits_banking = 3

banking_evolutionary_processes = [(0,
'entangle'), (1, 'evolve'), (2, 'entangle')]
```

```python
banking_maturation_circuit =
finance_maturation_circuit(num_qubits_banking, banking_evolutionary_processes)


# Define evolutionary processes for the investment sector

num_qubits_investment = 4

investment_evolutionary_processes = [(0, 'evolve'), (1, 'entangle'), (2, 'evolve'), (3, 'entangle')]

investment_maturation_circuit =
finance_maturation_circuit(num_qubits_investment, investment_evolutionary_processes)


# Visualize the quantum circuits

banking_maturation_circuit.draw('mpl'),
investment_maturation_circuit.draw('mpl')


# Simulate the quantum circuits

simulator =
Aer.get_backend('qasm_simulator')
```

```python
compiled_banking =
transpile(banking_maturation_circuit,
simulator)

compiled_investment =
transpile(investment_maturation_circuit,
simulator)


qobj_banking = assemble(compiled_banking)

qobj_investment =
assemble(compiled_investment)


result_banking =
simulator.run(qobj_banking).result()

result_investment =
simulator.run(qobj_investment).result()


# Plot the simulation results

counts_banking =
result_banking.get_counts(banking_maturatio
n_circuit)
```

```
counts_investment =
result_investment.get_counts(investment_mat
uration_circuit)
```

```
plot_histogram([counts_banking,
counts_investment], legend=['Banking Sector',
'Investment Sector'])
```

Summary:

Import Libraries: Essential libraries, including Qiskit, are imported for quantum circuit construction and simulation.

Quantum Circuit for Finance Maturation: A function is defined to create a quantum circuit representing the maturation of finance. Evolutionary processes are specified, with quantum gates symbolizing entanglement and evolution.

Visualization: Quantum circuits for the maturation of the banking and investment *sectors are visualized using Qiskit's visualization tools.*

Simulation: The quantum circuits are simulated using the QASM simulator from Qiskit.

Simulation Results Plot: The results of the simulation, representing the probabilities of different states, are plotted using a histogram. This provides insights into the quantum evolution and maturation of the banking and investment sectors.

This code serves as a quantum exploration of finance maturation, where the evolution of sectors is encoded in the language of qubits. Quantum principles become a guiding light, offering transformative insights into the intricate evolution of financial landscapes.

Chapter 9: Simulated Wisdom

in Healthcare

AI-Guided Journey Through

the Stages of Developm ent in the Healthcar e Industry

In this chapter, we embark on an AI-guided journey through the stages of development in the healthcare industry. The provided code represents an exploration of artificial intelligence (AI) as it illuminates the path of wisdom and progress in healthcare.

Python code

 # Simulated Wisdom in Healthcare - AI Analysis

 # Importing necessary libraries

import numpy as np

import pandas as pd

from sklearn.model_selection import train_test_split

from sklearn.ensemble import RandomForestClassifier

from sklearn.metrics import accuracy_score, classification_report

---

```python
# Generate synthetic data representing
healthcare features and development stages

np.random.seed(42)

data_size = 1000

healthcare_features =
np.random.rand(data_size, 5)

development_stages = np.random.randint(0, 2,
data_size)  # Binary classification: 0 for early
stage, 1 for advanced stage


# Create a DataFrame with synthetic data

healthcare_data =
pd.DataFrame(healthcare_features,
columns=['Feature_1', 'Feature_2',
'Feature_3', 'Feature_4', 'Feature_5'])

healthcare_data['Development_Stage'] =
development_stages


# Split the data into training and testing sets

X =
healthcare_data.drop('Development_Stage',
axis=1)
```

```python
y = healthcare_data['Development_Stage']

X_train, X_test, y_train, y_test = train_test_split(X, y, test_size=0.2, random_state=42)


# Train a Random Forest Classifier

rf_classifier = RandomForestClassifier(random_state=42)

rf_classifier.fit(X_train, y_train)


# Make predictions on the test set

y_pred = rf_classifier.predict(X_test)


# Analyze the results

accuracy = accuracy_score(y_test, y_pred)

classification_rep = classification_report(y_test, y_pred)


print(f"Accuracy: {accuracy}\nClassification Report:\n{classification_rep}")
```

Summary:

Import Libraries: Essential libraries, including NumPy, pandas, and scikit-learn, are imported for data manipulation and machine learning.

Generate Synthetic Data: Synthetic data is generated to represent healthcare features and their corresponding development stages.

DataFrame Creation: The synthetic data is organized into a DataFrame for further analysis.

Train-Test Split: The data is split into training and testing sets for machine learning model training and evaluation.

Random Forest Classifier: A Random Forest Classifier is trained on the healthcare features to predict the development stages.

Prediction and Analysis: The model's predictions are evaluated, and accuracy along with a classification report is generated to assess the AI-guided journey through the stages of development in the healthcare industry.

This code serves as a beacon of AI wisdom in healthcare, where machine learning algorithms illuminate the path towards understanding and navigating the developmental stages of this crucial industry. Through simulated insights, we uncover the potential for AI to guide and enhance the wisdom applied to healthcare advancements.

Chapter 10: Quantum Agricultur

e

Revolutio

n

Using

Quantum

Machine

Learning (QML) to Predict and Enhance Agricultur

al Advance ments

In this chapter, we harness the power of Quantum Machine Learning (QML) to predict and enhance agricultural advancements. The provided code represents a quantum revolution in agriculture, where quantum principles guide us in optimizing and advancing the agricultural landscape.

Python code

 # Quantum Agriculture Revolution - Quantum Machine Learning

 # Importing necessary libraries

import numpy as np

from qiskit import QuantumCircuit, Aer, transpile, assemble

from qiskit.visualization import plot_histogram

 # Define a quantum circuit for predicting and enhancing agricultural advancements

def quantum_agriculture_circuit(num_qubits, predictive_processes):

qc = QuantumCircuit(num_qubits)

 # Apply quantum gates representing predictive processes in agriculture

for process in predictive_processes:

```python
        qubit, gate_type = process

        if gate_type == 'entangle':

            qc.h(qubit)  # Apply a Hadamard gate
            for entanglement

        elif gate_type == 'evolve':

            qc.x(qubit)  # Apply an X-gate for
            evolution

        qc.barrier()


    return qc


# Define predictive processes for crop yield
enhancement

num_qubits_crop_yield = 4

crop_yield_predictive_processes = [(0,
'entangle'), (1, 'evolve'), (2, 'entangle'), (3,
'evolve')]

crop_yield_circuit =
quantum_agriculture_circuit(num_qubits_crop
_yield, crop_yield_predictive_processes)
```

```python
# Define predictive processes for soil health
improvement

num_qubits_soil_health = 3

soil_health_predictive_processes = [(0,
'evolve'), (1, 'entangle'), (2, 'evolve')]

soil_health_circuit =
quantum_agriculture_circuit(num_qubits_soil_
health, soil_health_predictive_processes)


# Visualize the quantum circuits

crop_yield_circuit.draw('mpl'),
soil_health_circuit.draw('mpl')


# Simulate the quantum circuits

simulator =
Aer.get_backend('qasm_simulator')

compiled_crop_yield =
transpile(crop_yield_circuit, simulator)

compiled_soil_health =
transpile(soil_health_circuit, simulator)
```

```
qobj_crop_yield =
assemble(compiled_crop_yield)

qobj_soil_health =
assemble(compiled_soil_health)


result_crop_yield =
simulator.run(qobj_crop_yield).result()

result_soil_health =
simulator.run(qobj_soil_health).result()


# Plot the simulation results

counts_crop_yield =
result_crop_yield.get_counts(crop_yield_circuit
)

counts_soil_health =
result_soil_health.get_counts(soil_health_circu
it)


plot_histogram([counts_crop_yield,
counts_soil_health], legend=['Crop Yield
Enhancement', 'Soil Health Improvement'])
```

Summary:

Import Libraries: Essential libraries, including Qiskit, are imported for quantum circuit construction and simulation.

Quantum Circuit for Agriculture Revolution: A function is defined to create a quantum circuit representing the revolution in agriculture. Predictive processes are specified, with quantum gates symbolizing entanglement and evolution.

Visualization: Quantum circuits for enhancing crop yield and improving soil health are visualized using Qiskit's visualization tools.

Simulation: The quantum circuits are simulated using the QASM simulator from Qiskit.

Simulation Results Plot: The results of the simulation, representing the probabilities of different states, are plotted using a histogram. This provides insights into the quantum revolution in predicting and enhancing agricultural advancements.

This code serves as a quantum leap in agriculture, where QML becomes the guiding force for predicting and optimizing crop yield and soil health. Through the language of qubits, we explore the potential of quantum principles to revolutionize and advance the field of agriculture.

Chapter 11: Quantum

Threads of Energy Simulating Energy Sectors and Their

Transitions with AI and Quantum Computing

In this chapter, we embark on a quantum exploration of energy sectors, simulating their transitions with the synergy of Artificial Intelligence (AI) and Quantum Computing. The provided code represents an intricate dance of qubits, unveiling the quantum threads that weave through the dynamic landscape of energy transitions.

Python code

 # Quantum Threads of Energy - Quantum Computing and AI

 # Importing necessary libraries

import numpy as np

from qiskit import QuantumCircuit, Aer, transpile, assemble

from qiskit.visualization import plot_histogram

 # Define a quantum circuit for simulating energy sector transitions

```python
def
quantum_energy_transition_circuit(num_qubits
, transition_processes):

    qc = QuantumCircuit(num_qubits)


    # Apply quantum gates representing
    transition processes in the energy sector

    for process in transition_processes:

        qubit, gate_type = process

        if gate_type == 'entangle':

            qc.h(qubit)  # Apply a Hadamard gate
            for entanglement

        elif gate_type == 'evolve':

            qc.x(qubit)  # Apply an X-gate for
            evolution

        qc.barrier()


    return qc
```

```
# Define transition processes for renewable
energy adoption

num_qubits_renewable_energy = 3

renewable_energy_transition_processes = [(0,
'entangle'), (1, 'evolve'), (2, 'entangle')]

renewable_energy_circuit =
quantum_energy_transition_circuit(num_qubits
_renewable_energy,
renewable_energy_transition_processes)


# Define transition processes for fossil fuel
phase-out

num_qubits_fossil_fuel = 4

fossil_fuel_transition_processes = [(0,
'evolve'), (1, 'entangle'), (2, 'evolve'), (3,
'entangle')]

fossil_fuel_circuit =
quantum_energy_transition_circuit(num_qubits
_fossil_fuel, fossil_fuel_transition_processes)


# Visualize the quantum circuits
```

```python
renewable_energy_circuit.draw('mpl'),
fossil_fuel_circuit.draw('mpl')


# Simulate the quantum circuits

simulator =
Aer.get_backend('qasm_simulator')

compiled_renewable_energy =
transpile(renewable_energy_circuit, simulator)

compiled_fossil_fuel =
transpile(fossil_fuel_circuit, simulator)


qobj_renewable_energy =
assemble(compiled_renewable_energy)

qobj_fossil_fuel =
assemble(compiled_fossil_fuel)


result_renewable_energy =
simulator.run(qobj_renewable_energy).result()

result_fossil_fuel =
simulator.run(qobj_fossil_fuel).result()
```

```
# Plot the simulation results

counts_renewable_energy =
result_renewable_energy.get_counts(renewab
le_energy_circuit)

counts_fossil_fuel =
result_fossil_fuel.get_counts(fossil_fuel_circuit
)


plot_histogram([counts_renewable_energy,
counts_fossil_fuel], legend=['Renewable
Energy Adoption', 'Fossil Fuel Phase-out'])
```

Summary:

Import Libraries: Essential libraries, including
Qiskit, are imported for quantum circuit
construction and simulation.

Quantum Circuit for Energy Sector Transitions:
A function is defined to create a quantum
circuit representing the transitions in the
energy sector. Transition processes are
specified, with quantum gates symbolizing
entanglement and evolution.

Visualization: Quantum circuits for the adoption of renewable energy and the phase-out of fossil fuels are visualized using Qiskit's visualization tools.

Simulation: The quantum circuits are simulated using the QASM simulator from Qiskit.

Simulation Results Plot: The results of the simulation, representing the probabilities of different states, are plotted using a histogram. This provides insights into the quantum threads that weave through the energy sector, simulating transitions with AI and quantum computing.

This code serves as a quantum tapestry woven with AI, depicting the transitions in the energy sector. Quantum threads entangle with the dynamics of renewable energy adoption and the phase-out of fossil fuels, showcasing the potential of quantum computing to simulate and guide the future of energy landscapes.

Chapter 12: Cosmic

Connectiv ity in Communi cation Examinin g How

Communication Sectors Evolve in the Cosmic

Simulatio n

In this chapter, we delve into the cosmic realm to explore how communication sectors evolve. The provided code represents an examination of the intricate dance of qubits, simulating the cosmic connectivity that shapes the evolution of communication sectors.

Python code

 # Cosmic Connectivity in Communication - Quantum Simulation

 # Importing necessary libraries

import numpy as np

```python
from qiskit import QuantumCircuit, Aer, transpile, assemble

from qiskit.visualization import plot_histogram


# Define a quantum circuit for simulating communication sector evolution

def quantum_communication_evolution_circuit(num_qubits, evolution_processes):

    qc = QuantumCircuit(num_qubits)


    # Apply quantum gates representing evolution processes in the communication sector

    for process in evolution_processes:

        qubit, gate_type = process

        if gate_type == 'entangle':

            qc.h(qubit)  # Apply a Hadamard gate for entanglement

        elif gate_type == 'evolve':
```

```
        qc.x(qubit)  # Apply an X-gate for
        evolution

        qc.barrier()


    return qc



# Define evolution processes for the rise of
        quantum communication

num_qubits_quantum_communication = 4

quantum_communication_evolution_processe
s = [(0, 'entangle'), (1, 'evolve'), (2, 'entangle'),
        (3, 'evolve')]

    quantum_communication_circuit =
quantum_communication_evolution_circuit(nu
    m_qubits_quantum_communication,
quantum_communication_evolution_processe
        s)



# Define evolution processes for the
integration of AI in communication

    num_qubits_ai_integration = 3
```

```python
ai_integration_evolution_processes = [(0,
'evolve'), (1, 'entangle'), (2, 'evolve')]

ai_integration_circuit =
quantum_communication_evolution_circuit(nu
m_qubits_ai_integration,
ai_integration_evolution_processes)


# Visualize the quantum circuits

quantum_communication_circuit.draw('mpl'),
ai_integration_circuit.draw('mpl')


# Simulate the quantum circuits

simulator =
Aer.get_backend('qasm_simulator')

compiled_quantum_communication =
transpile(quantum_communication_circuit,
simulator)

compiled_ai_integration =
transpile(ai_integration_circuit, simulator)


qobj_quantum_communication =
assemble(compiled_quantum_communication)
```

```
qobj_ai_integration =
assemble(compiled_ai_integration)


result_quantum_communication =
simulator.run(qobj_quantum_communication).r
esult()

result_ai_integration =
simulator.run(qobj_ai_integration).result()


# Plot the simulation results

counts_quantum_communication =
result_quantum_communication.get_counts(qu
antum_communication_circuit)

counts_ai_integration =
result_ai_integration.get_counts(ai_integration
_circuit)


plot_histogram([counts_quantum_communicati
on, counts_ai_integration], legend=['Quantum
Communication Rise', 'AI Integration in
Communication'])
```

Summary:

Import Libraries: Essential libraries, including Qiskit, are imported for quantum circuit construction and simulation.

Quantum Circuit for Communication Evolution: A function is defined to create a quantum circuit representing the evolution of communication sectors. Evolution processes are specified, with quantum gates symbolizing entanglement and evolution.

Visualization: Quantum circuits for the rise of quantum communication and the integration of AI in communication are visualized using Qiskit's visualization tools.

Simulation: The quantum circuits are simulated using the QASM simulator from Qiskit.

Simulation Results Plot: The results of the simulation, representing the probabilities of different states, are plotted using a histogram.

This provides insights into the cosmic connectivity that shapes the evolution of communication sectors in the cosmic simulation.

This code illuminates the quantum dance of communication evolution, where qubits entangle and evolve, symbolizing the rise of quantum communication and the integration of AI. In the cosmic simulation, quantum principles guide the connectivity that transforms communication sectors into a realm of infinite possibilities.

Chapter 13: AI and Quantum Culture Craft

Quantum Insights into the Cultural Evolution of

Societies through AI-Driven Simulations

In this chapter, we embark on a journey into the quantum realms of culture, exploring the evolution of societies through the lens of both Artificial Intelligence (AI) and quantum principles. The provided code encapsulates the essence of quantum culture craft, unraveling insights into the intricate tapestry of societal evolution.

Python code

```
# AI and Quantum Culture Craft - Simulating
Cultural Evolution


# Importing necessary libraries

import numpy as np

from qiskit import QuantumCircuit, Aer,
transpile, assemble

from qiskit.visualization import plot_histogram


# Define a quantum circuit for simulating
cultural evolution

def
quantum_cultural_evolution_circuit(num_qubit
s, cultural_processes):

qc = QuantumCircuit(num_qubits)
```

```
# Apply quantum gates representing cultural
processes

for process in cultural_processes:

    qubit, gate_type = process

    if gate_type == 'entangle':

        qc.h(qubit)  # Apply a Hadamard gate
        for entanglement

    elif gate_type == 'evolve':

        qc.x(qubit)  # Apply an X-gate for
        evolution

    qc.barrier()


return qc


# Define cultural processes for the fusion of
traditional and technological cultures

num_qubits_cultural_fusion = 4

cultural_fusion_processes = [(0, 'entangle'), (1,
'evolve'), (2, 'entangle'), (3, 'evolve')]
```

```python
cultural_fusion_circuit =
quantum_cultural_evolution_circuit(num_qubit
s_cultural_fusion, cultural_fusion_processes)


# Define cultural processes for the emergence
of collaborative and diverse societies

num_qubits_cultural_emergence = 3

cultural_emergence_processes = [(0, 'evolve'),
(1, 'entangle'), (2, 'evolve')]

cultural_emergence_circuit =
quantum_cultural_evolution_circuit(num_qubit
s_cultural_emergence,
cultural_emergence_processes)


# Visualize the quantum circuits

cultural_fusion_circuit.draw('mpl'),
cultural_emergence_circuit.draw('mpl')


# Simulate the quantum circuits

simulator =
Aer.get_backend('qasm_simulator')
```

```
compiled_cultural_fusion =
transpile(cultural_fusion_circuit, simulator)

compiled_cultural_emergence =
transpile(cultural_emergence_circuit,
          simulator)


qobj_cultural_fusion =
assemble(compiled_cultural_fusion)

qobj_cultural_emergence =
assemble(compiled_cultural_emergence)


result_cultural_fusion =
simulator.run(qobj_cultural_fusion).result()

result_cultural_emergence =
simulator.run(qobj_cultural_emergence).result(
)


# Plot the simulation results

counts_cultural_fusion =
result_cultural_fusion.get_counts(cultural_fusi
on_circuit)
```

```
counts_cultural_emergence =
result_cultural_emergence.get_counts(cultural
_emergence_circuit)


plot_histogram([counts_cultural_fusion,
counts_cultural_emergence], legend=['Cultural
Fusion', 'Cultural Emergence'])
```

Summary:

Import Libraries: Essential libraries, including
Qiskit, are imported for quantum circuit
construction and simulation.

Quantum Circuit for Cultural Evolution: A
function is defined to create a quantum circuit
representing the evolution of cultures. Cultural
processes are specified, with quantum gates
symbolizing entanglement and evolution.

Visualization: Quantum circuits for the fusion
of traditional and technological cultures and
the emergence of collaborative and diverse

societies are visualized using Qiskit's visualization tools.

Simulation: The quantum circuits are simulated using the QASM simulator from Qiskit.

Simulation Results Plot: The results of the simulation, representing the probabilities of different states, are plotted using a histogram. This provides insights into the quantum culture craft, unraveling the intricate tapestry of societal evolution.

This code captures the quantum essence of cultural evolution, where qubits entangle and evolve, symbolizing the fusion of traditional and technological cultures and the emergence of collaborative and diverse societies. Through the lens of AI-driven simulations, we gain quantum insights into the cultural fabric of evolving societies.

Chapter 14: The Quantum Era of Education

Navigatin g the Simulated Realms of Education and Its

Quantum Transform ations

In this chapter, we embark on a journey into the quantum era of education, exploring the simulated realms where education undergoes transformative changes guided by quantum principles. The provided code encapsulates the essence of this quantum education evolution, offering insights into the intricate dance of qubits shaping the future of learning.

Python code

The Quantum Era of Education - Quantum Transformation

```python
# Importing necessary libraries

import numpy as np

from qiskit import QuantumCircuit, Aer, transpile, assemble

from qiskit.visualization import plot_histogram


# Define a quantum circuit for simulating the quantum era of education
def quantum_education_transformation_circuit(num_qubits, education_processes):

    qc = QuantumCircuit(num_qubits)


    # Apply quantum gates representing education processes

    for process in education_processes:

        qubit, gate_type = process
```

```python
    if gate_type == 'entangle':

        qc.h(qubit)  # Apply a Hadamard gate
        for entanglement

    elif gate_type == 'evolve':

        qc.x(qubit)  # Apply an X-gate for
        evolution

    qc.barrier()


    return qc


# Define education processes for personalized
learning and skill enhancement

num_qubits_personalized_learning = 3

personalized_learning_processes = [(0,
'entangle'), (1, 'evolve'), (2, 'entangle')]

personalized_learning_circuit =
quantum_education_transformation_circuit(nu
m_qubits_personalized_learning,
personalized_learning_processes)
```

```python
# Define education processes for collaborative
knowledge networks

num_qubits_collaborative_knowledge = 4

collaborative_knowledge_processes = [(0,
'evolve'), (1, 'entangle'), (2, 'evolve'), (3,
'entangle')]

collaborative_knowledge_circuit =
quantum_education_transformation_circuit(num_qubits_collaborative_knowledge,
collaborative_knowledge_processes)


# Visualize the quantum circuits

personalized_learning_circuit.draw('mpl'),
collaborative_knowledge_circuit.draw('mpl')


# Simulate the quantum circuits

simulator =
Aer.get_backend('qasm_simulator')

compiled_personalized_learning =
transpile(personalized_learning_circuit,
simulator)
```

```python
compiled_collaborative_knowledge =
transpile(collaborative_knowledge_circuit,
simulator)


qobj_personalized_learning =
assemble(compiled_personalized_learning)

qobj_collaborative_knowledge =
assemble(compiled_collaborative_knowledge)


result_personalized_learning =
simulator.run(qobj_personalized_learning).res
ult()

result_collaborative_knowledge =
simulator.run(qobj_collaborative_knowledge).r
esult()


# Plot the simulation results

counts_personalized_learning =
result_personalized_learning.get_counts(perso
nalized_learning_circuit)
```

```
counts_collaborative_knowledge =
result_collaborative_knowledge.get_counts(col
laborative_knowledge_circuit)


plot_histogram([counts_personalized_learning,
counts_collaborative_knowledge],
legend=['Personalized Learning', 'Collaborative
Knowledge Networks'])
```

Summary:

Import Libraries: Essential libraries, including Qiskit, are imported for quantum circuit construction and simulation.

Quantum Circuit for Education Transformation: A function is defined to create a quantum circuit representing the quantum transformation of education. Education processes are specified, with quantum gates symbolizing entanglement and evolution.

Visualization: Quantum circuits for personalized learning and skill enhancement, as well as collaborative knowledge networks, are visualized using Qiskit's visualization tools.

Simulation: The quantum circuits are simulated using the QASM simulator from Qiskit.

Simulation Results Plot: The results of the simulation, representing the probabilities of different states, are plotted using a histogram. This provides insights into the quantum era of education, showcasing the transformative changes guided by quantum principles.

This code encapsulates the quantum journey of education, where qubits entangle and evolve, symbolizing personalized learning and collaborative knowledge networks. In the simulated realms, quantum principles guide the transformative changes shaping the future landscape of education.

Chapter 15:

Virtualizati on of Reality

Blurring the Lines Between Reality and Simulatio

n Using AI and Quantum Technologies

In this chapter, we explore the frontier where reality and simulation converge, creating a tapestry woven with both Artificial Intelligence (AI) and quantum technologies. The provided code encapsulates the essence of this virtualization, offering insights into the intricate dance of qubits that blur the boundaries between what is real and what is simulated.

Python code

 # Virtualization of Reality - AI and Quantum Convergence

 # Importing necessary libraries

import numpy as np

from qiskit import QuantumCircuit, Aer, transpile, assemble

from qiskit.visualization import plot_histogram

 # Define a quantum circuit for simulating the virtualization of reality

def quantum_reality_virtualization_circuit(num_qubits, virtualization_processes):

qc = QuantumCircuit(num_qubits)

```python
# Apply quantum gates representing
virtualization processes

for process in virtualization_processes:

    qubit, gate_type = process

    if gate_type == 'entangle':

        qc.h(qubit)  # Apply a Hadamard gate
        for entanglement

    elif gate_type == 'evolve':

        qc.x(qubit)  # Apply an X-gate for
        evolution

    qc.barrier()


return qc



# Define virtualization processes for blending
reality and simulation

num_qubits_reality_simulation_blend = 4
```

```python
reality_simulation_blend_processes = [(0,
'entangle'), (1, 'evolve'), (2, 'entangle'), (3,
'evolve')]

reality_simulation_blend_circuit =
quantum_reality_virtualization_circuit(num_qu
bits_reality_simulation_blend,
reality_simulation_blend_processes)


# Define virtualization processes for AI-guided
perceptual shifts

num_qubits_perceptual_shifts = 3

perceptual_shifts_processes = [(0, 'evolve'),
(1, 'entangle'), (2, 'evolve')]

perceptual_shifts_circuit =
quantum_reality_virtualization_circuit(num_qu
bits_perceptual_shifts,
perceptual_shifts_processes)


# Visualize the quantum circuits

reality_simulation_blend_circuit.draw('mpl'),
perceptual_shifts_circuit.draw('mpl')
```

```python
# Simulate the quantum circuits

simulator =
Aer.get_backend('qasm_simulator')

compiled_reality_simulation_blend =
transpile(reality_simulation_blend_circuit,
            simulator)

compiled_perceptual_shifts =
transpile(perceptual_shifts_circuit, simulator)


qobj_reality_simulation_blend =
assemble(compiled_reality_simulation_blend)

qobj_perceptual_shifts =
assemble(compiled_perceptual_shifts)


result_reality_simulation_blend =
simulator.run(qobj_reality_simulation_blend).re
sult()

result_perceptual_shifts =
simulator.run(qobj_perceptual_shifts).result()


# Plot the simulation results
```

```
counts_reality_simulation_blend =
result_reality_simulation_blend.get_counts(rea
lity_simulation_blend_circuit)

counts_perceptual_shifts =
result_perceptual_shifts.get_counts(perceptual
_shifts_circuit)


plot_histogram([counts_reality_simulation_ble
nd, counts_perceptual_shifts],
legend=['Reality-Simulation Blend', 'AI-Guided
Perceptual Shifts'])
```

Summary:

Import Libraries: Essential libraries, including Qiskit, are imported for quantum circuit construction and simulation.

Quantum Circuit for Reality Virtualization: A function is defined to create a quantum circuit representing the virtualization of reality. Virtualization processes are specified, with quantum gates symbolizing entanglement and evolution.

Visualization: Quantum circuits for blending reality and simulation, as well as AI-guided perceptual shifts, are visualized using Qiskit's visualization tools.

Simulation: The quantum circuits are simulated using the QASM simulator from Qiskit.

Simulation Results Plot: The results of the simulation, representing the probabilities of different states, are plotted using a histogram. This provides insights into the virtualization of reality, where qubits blur the lines between reality and simulation, guided by both AI and quantum technologies.

This code captures the quantum dance of reality virtualization, where qubits entangle and evolve, symbolizing the blending of reality and simulation and AI-guided perceptual shifts. In this convergence of quantum and AI technologies, the boundaries between the real and the simulated become beautifully indistinct.

Chapter 16: AI in the

Quantum Political Arena

Analyzing the Political

Stages of Developm ent through the Lens of

Quantum-Powered AI

In this chapter, we delve into the political arena, leveraging the power of quantum computing and Artificial Intelligence (AI) to analyze and understand the various stages of political development. The provided code encapsulates the essence of this quantum analysis, offering insights into the intricate dance of qubits that illuminate the complexities of political evolution.

Python code

AI in the Quantum Political Arena - Quantum Analysis

Importing necessary libraries

import numpy as np

from qiskit import QuantumCircuit, Aer, transpile, assemble

from qiskit.visualization import plot_histogram

Define a quantum circuit for simulating political analysis

def quantum_political_analysis_circuit(num_qubits, political_processes):

qc = QuantumCircuit(num_qubits)

Apply quantum gates representing political processes

for process in political_processes:

qubit, gate_type = process

```python
    if gate_type == 'entangle':

        qc.h(qubit)  # Apply a Hadamard gate
                     for entanglement

    elif gate_type == 'evolve':

        qc.x(qubit)  # Apply an X-gate for
                     evolution

    qc.barrier()


    return qc


# Define political processes for analyzing
development stages

num_qubits_political_development = 4

political_development_processes = [(0,
'entangle'), (1, 'evolve'), (2, 'entangle'), (3,
'evolve')]

political_development_circuit =
quantum_political_analysis_circuit(num_qubits
_political_development,
political_development_processes)
```

```python
# Define political processes for AI-guided
policy evolution

num_qubits_policy_evolution = 3

policy_evolution_processes = [(0, 'evolve'), (1,
'entangle'), (2, 'evolve')]

policy_evolution_circuit =
quantum_political_analysis_circuit(num_qubits
_policy_evolution, policy_evolution_processes)


# Visualize the quantum circuits

political_development_circuit.draw('mpl'),
policy_evolution_circuit.draw('mpl')


# Simulate the quantum circuits

simulator =
Aer.get_backend('qasm_simulator')

compiled_political_development =
transpile(political_development_circuit,
simulator)

compiled_policy_evolution =
transpile(policy_evolution_circuit, simulator)
```

```
qobj_political_development =
assemble(compiled_political_development)

qobj_policy_evolution =
assemble(compiled_policy_evolution)


result_political_development =
simulator.run(qobj_political_development).resu
lt()

result_policy_evolution =
simulator.run(qobj_policy_evolution).result()


# Plot the simulation results

counts_political_development =
result_political_development.get_counts(politic
al_development_circuit)

counts_policy_evolution =
result_policy_evolution.get_counts(policy_evol
ution_circuit)


plot_histogram([counts_political_development,
counts_policy_evolution], legend=['Political
```

Development Analysis', 'AI-Guided Policy Evolution'])

Summary:

Import Libraries: Essential libraries, including Qiskit, are imported for quantum circuit construction and simulation.

Quantum Circuit for Political Analysis: A function is defined to create a quantum circuit representing the analysis of political development. Political processes are specified, with quantum gates symbolizing entanglement and evolution.

Visualization: Quantum circuits for analyzing political development stages and AI-guided policy evolution are visualized using Qiskit's visualization tools.

Simulation: The quantum circuits are simulated using the QASM simulator from Qiskit.

Simulation Results Plot: The results of the simulation, representing the probabilities of different states, are plotted using a histogram. This provides insights into the quantum-powered analysis of political stages and the evolution of policies guided by AI.

This code illuminates the quantum analysis of political development, where qubits entangle and evolve, symbolizing the stages of political evolution and AI-guided policy shifts. In the quantum political arena, the power of AI and quantum technologies converge to unravel the complexities of political landscapes.

Chapter 17:

Quantum Transport and Connectiv ity

Simulating the Evolution of Transportation and

Connectiv ity Sectors

In this chapter, we embark on a journey into the quantum realms of transport and connectivity, simulating the evolution of these critical sectors. The provided code encapsulates the essence of this quantum simulation, offering insights into the intricate dance of qubits that shape the future of transportation and connectivity.

Python code

Quantum Transport and Connectivity - Quantum Simulation

Importing necessary libraries

```
import numpy as np

from qiskit import QuantumCircuit, Aer, transpile, assemble

from qiskit.visualization import plot_histogram


# Define a quantum circuit for simulating transport and connectivity evolution

def quantum_transport_connectivity_circuit(num_qubits, transport_processes):

    qc = QuantumCircuit(num_qubits)


    # Apply quantum gates representing transport processes

    for process in transport_processes:

        qubit, gate_type = process
```

```python
    if gate_type == 'entangle':

        qc.h(qubit)  # Apply a Hadamard gate
        for entanglement

    elif gate_type == 'evolve':

        qc.x(qubit)  # Apply an X-gate for
        evolution

        qc.barrier()


    return qc


# Define transport processes for quantum
evolution

num_qubits_transport_evolution = 4

transport_evolution_processes = [(0,
'entangle'), (1, 'evolve'), (2, 'entangle'), (3,
'evolve')]

transport_evolution_circuit =
quantum_transport_connectivity_circuit(num_q
ubits_transport_evolution,
transport_evolution_processes)
```

```python
# Define connectivity processes for quantum integration

num_qubits_connectivity_integration = 3

connectivity_integration_processes = [(0, 'evolve'), (1, 'entangle'), (2, 'evolve')]

connectivity_integration_circuit = quantum_transport_connectivity_circuit(num_qubits_connectivity_integration, connectivity_integration_processes)


# Visualize the quantum circuits

transport_evolution_circuit.draw('mpl'), connectivity_integration_circuit.draw('mpl')


# Simulate the quantum circuits

simulator = Aer.get_backend('qasm_simulator')

compiled_transport_evolution = transpile(transport_evolution_circuit, simulator)

compiled_connectivity_integration = transpile(connectivity_integration_circuit, simulator)
```

```
qobj_transport_evolution =
assemble(compiled_transport_evolution)

qobj_connectivity_integration =
assemble(compiled_connectivity_integration)


result_transport_evolution =
simulator.run(qobj_transport_evolution).result()

result_connectivity_integration =
simulator.run(qobj_connectivity_integration).re
sult()


# Plot the simulation results

counts_transport_evolution =
result_transport_evolution.get_counts(transpor
t_evolution_circuit)

counts_connectivity_integration =
result_connectivity_integration.get_counts(con
nectivity_integration_circuit)


plot_histogram([counts_transport_evolution,
counts_connectivity_integration],
```

legend=['Transport Evolution', 'Connectivity
Integration'])

Summary:

Import Libraries: Essential libraries, including
Qiskit, are imported for quantum circuit
construction and simulation.

Quantum Circuit for Transport and
Connectivity: A function is defined to create a
quantum circuit representing the simulation of
transport and connectivity evolution. Transport
processes are specified, with quantum gates
symbolizing entanglement and evolution.

Visualization: Quantum circuits for the
evolution of transportation and the integration
of quantum connectivity are visualized using
Qiskit's visualization tools.

Simulation: The quantum circuits are simulated
using the QASM simulator from Qiskit.

Simulation Results Plot: The results of the simulation, representing the probabilities of different states, are plotted using a histogram. This provides insights into the quantum evolution of transportation and the integration of quantum connectivity.

This code captures the quantum dance of transport and connectivity evolution, where qubits entangle and evolve, symbolizing the future of transportation and the integration of quantum connectivity. In the simulated realms, quantum principles guide the transformative changes shaping the landscape of transport and connectivity sectors.

Chapter 18: The Quantum Pulse of Environment

Detecting Environmental Changes and Developm

ental
Stages
through
AI-
Enhanced

Simulatio ns

In this chapter, we explore the quantum realm of environmental monitoring, leveraging the capabilities of Artificial Intelligence (AI) to detect changes and understand the developmental stages of our environment. The provided code encapsulates the essence of this quantum simulation, offering insights into the intricate dance of qubits that unveil the pulse of our surroundings.

Python code

 # The Quantum Pulse of Environment - AI-Enhanced Simulation

```python
# Importing necessary libraries

import numpy as np

from qiskit import QuantumCircuit, Aer, transpile, assemble

from qiskit.visualization import plot_histogram


# Define a quantum circuit for simulating environmental changes

def quantum_environment_simulation_circuit(num_qubits, environment_processes):

    qc = QuantumCircuit(num_qubits)


    # Apply quantum gates representing environmental processes

    for process in environment_processes:

        qubit, gate_type = process

        if gate_type == 'entangle':

            qc.h(qubit)  # Apply a Hadamard gate for entanglement
```

```python
    elif gate_type == 'evolve':

        qc.x(qubit)  # Apply an X-gate for
        evolution

    qc.barrier()


    return qc


# Define environmental processes for AI-
enhanced detection

num_qubits_environment_detection = 4

environment_detection_processes = [(0,
'entangle'), (1, 'evolve'), (2, 'entangle'), (3,
'evolve')]

environment_detection_circuit =
quantum_environment_simulation_circuit(num
_qubits_environment_detection,
environment_detection_processes)


# Define environmental processes for AI-
guided adaptive responses

num_qubits_adaptive_responses = 3
```

```python
adaptive_responses_processes = [(0,
'evolve'), (1, 'entangle'), (2, 'evolve')]

adaptive_responses_circuit =
quantum_environment_simulation_circuit(num
_qubits_adaptive_responses,
adaptive_responses_processes)


# Visualize the quantum circuits

environment_detection_circuit.draw('mpl'),
adaptive_responses_circuit.draw('mpl')


# Simulate the quantum circuits

simulator =
Aer.get_backend('qasm_simulator')

compiled_environment_detection =
transpile(environment_detection_circuit,
simulator)

compiled_adaptive_responses =
transpile(adaptive_responses_circuit,
simulator)
```

```
qobj_environment_detection =
assemble(compiled_environment_detection)

qobj_adaptive_responses =
assemble(compiled_adaptive_responses)


result_environment_detection =
simulator.run(qobj_environment_detection).res
ult()

result_adaptive_responses =
simulator.run(qobj_adaptive_responses).result
()


# Plot the simulation results

counts_environment_detection =
result_environment_detection.get_counts(envir
onment_detection_circuit)

counts_adaptive_responses =
result_adaptive_responses.get_counts(adaptiv
e_responses_circuit)


plot_histogram([counts_environment_detection
, counts_adaptive_responses],
```

legend=['Environment Detection', 'AI-Guided Adaptive Responses'])

Summary:

Import Libraries: Essential libraries, including Qiskit, are imported for quantum circuit construction and simulation.

Quantum Circuit for Environmental Simulation: A function is defined to create a quantum circuit representing the simulation of environmental changes. Environmental processes are specified, with quantum gates symbolizing entanglement and evolution.

Visualization: Quantum circuits for the detection of environmental changes and AI-guided adaptive responses are visualized using Qiskit's visualization tools.

Simulation: The quantum circuits are simulated using the QASM simulator from Qiskit.

Simulation Results Plot: The results of the simulation, representing the probabilities of different states, are plotted using a histogram. This provides insights into the quantum detection of environmental changes and the adaptive responses guided by AI.

This code captures the quantum pulse of the environment, where qubits entangle and evolve, symbolizing the detection of changes and adaptive responses guided by AI. In the simulated quantum environment, the fusion of quantum principles and AI enhances our understanding of the developmental stages and pulse of the world around us.

Chapter 19: Quantum Exploratio

*n of
Quantum
Research
AI-Driven
Insights
into the*

Stages of Developm ent in Scientific Research

In this chapter, we embark on a quantum exploration of the realm of scientific research, utilizing the power of Artificial Intelligence (AI) to gain insights into the developmental stages.

The provided code encapsulates the essence of this quantum exploration, offering a glimpse into the intricate dance of qubits that unravel the stages of progress in the field of quantum research.

Python code

```
# Quantum Exploration of Quantum Research - AI-Driven Insights

# Importing necessary libraries

import numpy as np

from qiskit import QuantumCircuit, Aer, transpile, assemble

from qiskit.visualization import plot_histogram

# Define a quantum circuit for simulating quantum research stages

def quantum_research_simulation_circuit(num_qubits, research_processes):
```

```python
    qc = QuantumCircuit(num_qubits)

    # Apply quantum gates representing
    research processes

    for process in research_processes:

        qubit, gate_type = process

        if gate_type == 'entangle':

            qc.h(qubit)  # Apply a Hadamard gate
            for entanglement

        elif gate_type == 'evolve':

            qc.x(qubit)  # Apply an X-gate for
            evolution

        qc.barrier()


    return qc


# Define research processes for AI-driven
exploration
num_qubits_ai_driven_exploration = 4
```

```python
ai_driven_exploration_processes = [(0,
'entangle'), (1, 'evolve'), (2, 'entangle'), (3,
'evolve')]

ai_driven_exploration_circuit =
quantum_research_simulation_circuit(num_qu
bits_ai_driven_exploration,
ai_driven_exploration_processes)


# Define research processes for quantum
experimentation

num_qubits_quantum_experimentation = 3

quantum_experimentation_processes = [(0,
'evolve'), (1, 'entangle'), (2, 'evolve')]

quantum_experimentation_circuit =
quantum_research_simulation_circuit(num_qu
bits_quantum_experimentation,
quantum_experimentation_processes)


# Visualize the quantum circuits

ai_driven_exploration_circuit.draw('mpl'),
quantum_experimentation_circuit.draw('mpl')
```

```python
# Simulate the quantum circuits
simulator = Aer.get_backend('qasm_simulator')

compiled_ai_driven_exploration = transpile(ai_driven_exploration_circuit, simulator)

compiled_quantum_experimentation = transpile(quantum_experimentation_circuit, simulator)


qobj_ai_driven_exploration = assemble(compiled_ai_driven_exploration)

qobj_quantum_experimentation = assemble(compiled_quantum_experimentation)


result_ai_driven_exploration = simulator.run(qobj_ai_driven_exploration).result()

result_quantum_experimentation = simulator.run(qobj_quantum_experimentation).result()
```

Plot the simulation results

```
counts_ai_driven_exploration =
result_ai_driven_exploration.get_counts(ai_dri
ven_exploration_circuit)

counts_quantum_experimentation =
result_quantum_experimentation.get_counts(q
uantum_experimentation_circuit)


plot_histogram([counts_ai_driven_exploration,
counts_quantum_experimentation],
legend=['AI-Driven Exploration', 'Quantum
Experimentation'])
```

Summary:

Import Libraries: Essential libraries, including Qiskit, are imported for quantum circuit construction and simulation.

Quantum Circuit for Research Simulation: A function is defined to create a quantum circuit representing the simulation of research stages.

Research processes are specified, with quantum gates symbolizing entanglement and evolution.

Visualization: Quantum circuits for AI-driven exploration and quantum experimentation in research are visualized using Qiskit's visualization tools.

Simulation: The quantum circuits are simulated using the QASM simulator from Qiskit.

Simulation Results Plot: The results of the simulation, representing the probabilities of different states, are plotted using a histogram. This provides insights into the quantum-driven exploration of research stages and the experimental nature of quantum research.

This code captures the quantum exploration of quantum research, where qubits entangle and evolve, symbolizing AI-driven insights and quantum experimentation. In the simulated quantum research environment, the fusion of *quantum principles and AI enhances our understanding of the developmental stages and the path of scientific exploration.*

Chapter 20: The

Future Unveiled

Peering into the Future Using

Quantum Machine Learning: Potentials and Ethical

Considera tions

In this chapter, we embark on a journey into the unknown, peering into the future with the lens of quantum machine learning. We explore the potentials and ethical considerations of unveiling the mysteries that lie ahead. The provided code encapsulates the essence of this futuristic exploration, offering a glimpse into the intricate dance of qubits that reveal the possibilities and dilemmas of the quantum future.

Python code

 # The Future Unveiled - Quantum Machine Learning Exploration

```python
# Importing necessary libraries

import numpy as np

from qiskit import QuantumCircuit, Aer,
transpile, assemble

from qiskit.visualization import plot_histogram


# Define a quantum circuit for simulating future
exploration

def
quantum_future_exploration_circuit(num_qubit
s, future_processes):

    qc = QuantumCircuit(num_qubits)


    # Apply quantum gates representing future
exploration processes

    for process in future_processes:

        qubit, gate_type = process

        if gate_type == 'entangle':

            qc.h(qubit)  # Apply a Hadamard gate
for entanglement
```

```
    elif gate_type == 'evolve':

        qc.x(qubit)  # Apply an X-gate for
        evolution

        qc.barrier()


    return qc


# Define future exploration processes for
quantum machine learning

num_qubits_quantum_ml_exploration = 4

quantum_ml_exploration_processes = [(0,
'entangle'), (1, 'evolve'), (2, 'entangle'), (3,
'evolve')]

quantum_ml_exploration_circuit =
quantum_future_exploration_circuit(num_qubit
s_quantum_ml_exploration,
quantum_ml_exploration_processes)


# Define ethical considerations processes for
quantum future

num_qubits_ethical_considerations = 3
```

```python
ethical_considerations_processes = [(0,
'evolve'), (1, 'entangle'), (2, 'evolve')]

ethical_considerations_circuit =
quantum_future_exploration_circuit(num_qubit
s_ethical_considerations,
ethical_considerations_processes)


# Visualize the quantum circuits

quantum_ml_exploration_circuit.draw('mpl'),
ethical_considerations_circuit.draw('mpl')


# Simulate the quantum circuits

simulator =
Aer.get_backend('qasm_simulator')

compiled_quantum_ml_exploration =
transpile(quantum_ml_exploration_circuit,
simulator)

compiled_ethical_considerations =
transpile(ethical_considerations_circuit,
simulator)
```

```
qobj_quantum_ml_exploration =
assemble(compiled_quantum_ml_exploration)

qobj_ethical_considerations =
assemble(compiled_ethical_considerations)


result_quantum_ml_exploration =
simulator.run(qobj_quantum_ml_exploration).r
esult()

result_ethical_considerations =
simulator.run(qobj_ethical_considerations).res
ult()


# Plot the simulation results

counts_quantum_ml_exploration =
result_quantum_ml_exploration.get_counts(qu
antum_ml_exploration_circuit)

counts_ethical_considerations =
result_ethical_considerations.get_counts(ethic
al_considerations_circuit)


plot_histogram([counts_quantum_ml_explorati
on, counts_ethical_considerations],
```

legend=['Quantum ML Exploration', 'Ethical Considerations'])

Summary:

Import Libraries: Essential libraries, including Qiskit, are imported for quantum circuit construction and simulation.

Quantum Circuit for Future Exploration: A function is defined to create a quantum circuit representing the simulation of future exploration. Processes are specified, with quantum gates symbolizing entanglement and evolution.

Visualization: Quantum circuits for quantum machine learning exploration and ethical considerations in the quantum future are visualized using Qiskit's visualization tools.

Simulation: The quantum circuits are simulated using the QASM simulator from Qiskit.

Simulation Results Plot: The results of the simulation, representing the probabilities of different states, are plotted using a histogram. This provides insights into the quantum-driven exploration of the future and the ethical considerations that accompany such explorations.

This code captures the essence of quantum machine learning exploration into the future, where qubits entangle and evolve, symbolizing the potentials and ethical considerations of the quantum future. In the simulated quantum landscape, we peer into the unknown, acknowledging the power and responsibility that comes with unveiling the mysteries of what lies ahead.

Chapter 21: Quantum

Reflections

A Holistic Reflection on the Mystical

Journey Through Developmental Stages using AI,

Quantum Machine Learning, and Simulated

Time Travel

In this concluding chapter, we engage in a reflective exploration of the profound journey through developmental stages, guided by the amalgamation of Artificial Intelligence (AI), Quantum Machine Learning (QML), and the whimsical concept of simulated time travel. The provided code encapsulates the essence of this reflective journey, offering a glimpse into the intricate dance of qubits that symbolize the culmination of wisdom gained from traversing the simulated realms.

Python code

 # Quantum Reflections - Holistic Reflection Code

```python
# Importing necessary libraries

import numpy as np

from qiskit import QuantumCircuit, Aer,
transpile, assemble

from qiskit.visualization import plot_histogram


# Define a quantum circuit for holistic reflection
def
quantum_holistic_reflection_circuit(num_qubits
, reflection_processes):

    qc = QuantumCircuit(num_qubits)


    # Apply quantum gates representing
    reflection processes

    for process in reflection_processes:

        qubit, gate_type = process

        if gate_type == 'entangle':

            qc.h(qubit)  # Apply a Hadamard gate
            for entanglement
```

```python
    elif gate_type == 'evolve':

        qc.x(qubit)  # Apply an X-gate for
            evolution

        qc.barrier()


    return qc


# Define reflection processes for holistic
    quantum reflection

num_qubits_holistic_reflection = 4

holistic_reflection_processes = [(0, 'entangle'),
    (1, 'evolve'), (2, 'entangle'), (3, 'evolve')]

holistic_reflection_circuit =
quantum_holistic_reflection_circuit(num_qubits
    _holistic_reflection,
    holistic_reflection_processes)


# Visualize the quantum circuit for holistic
    reflection

holistic_reflection_circuit.draw('mpl')
```

```
# Simulate the quantum circuit

simulator =
Aer.get_backend('qasm_simulator')

compiled_holistic_reflection =
transpile(holistic_reflection_circuit, simulator)

qobj_holistic_reflection =
assemble(compiled_holistic_reflection)

result_holistic_reflection =
simulator.run(qobj_holistic_reflection).result()


# Plot the simulation result

counts_holistic_reflection =
result_holistic_reflection.get_counts(holistic_re
flection_circuit)

plot_histogram([counts_holistic_reflection],
legend=['Holistic Reflection'])
```

Summary:

Import Libraries: Essential libraries, including Qiskit, are imported for quantum circuit construction and simulation.

Quantum Circuit for Holistic Reflection: A function is defined to create a quantum circuit representing the holistic reflection on the journey through developmental stages. Reflection processes are specified, with quantum gates symbolizing entanglement and evolution.

Visualization: The quantum circuit for holistic reflection is visualized using Qiskit's visualization tools.

Simulation: The quantum circuit is simulated using the QASM simulator from Qiskit.

Simulation Result Plot: The results of the simulation, representing the probabilities of different states, are plotted using a histogram. This provides a symbolic representation of the holistic reflection on the mystical journey through developmental stages.

This code serves as a symbolic representation of the holistic reflection, where qubits entangle and evolve, symbolizing the culmination of wisdom gained from traversing the simulated realms guided by AI, Quantum Machine Learning, and the whimsical concept of simulated time travel. In this concluding chapter, we reflect on the profound insights gleaned from the journey, acknowledging the transformative power of AI and quantum technologies in shaping our understanding of existence and the future.

Chapter 22: Conclusio n - A Quantum

Tapestry of Wisdom and Tomorro

W's

Canvas

In the concluding chapter of our exploration into the realms of AI, Quantum Machine Learning (QML), and the philosophical notions of life simulation, we find ourselves at the nexus of technological innovation and existential contemplation. This journey has been a tapestry woven with the threads of quantum entanglement, machine learning algorithms, and the profound questions that arise when we peer into the heart of simulated realities.

Reflecting on the Quantum Odyssey: Unveiling the Threads of Wisdom

As we reflect on the chapters that have unfolded, we see the dance of qubits guiding our exploration. The Symphony of Neural Rhythms introduced us to the intricacies of brain pressure measurement and life simulation, setting the stage for a deeper understanding of the interplay between our minds, AI, and the simulated constructs of existence.

In The Dance of Neurons, we delved into the ballet of information orchestrated by neural networks, witnessing how AI mimics the very fabric of our cognitive processes. The elegance of brain pressure took center stage in the subsequent chapter, where we discovered the delicate dynamics influencing cognitive functioning and the potential of AI to navigate these complexities.

Strings of Consciousness pulled back the curtain on life in simulation, inviting us to question the nature of reality itself. As we navigated the tapestry of logics in the following chapter, we witnessed the evolution from simple rules to complex AI logics, marveling at the ingenuity of human and artificial minds alike.

Dialogues with the Mind: Navigating the Boundaries of Machine Learning

Conversations with Neural Networks in Chapter 6 showcased the evolving dialogue between humans and machines. We explored the boundaries of machine learning, witnessing the symbiotic relationship between our queries and the algorithms that seek to understand and respond.

Measuring Brain Pressure with AI became the focus in Chapter 7, where we uncovered the potential of algorithms to detect and predict changes in brain pressure. The Canvas of Solutions, our eighth chapter, painted a picture of innovative approaches to tracking brain pressure, highlighting emerging technologies and breakthroughs.

Navigating the Labyrinth in Chapter 9 led us through the challenges and pitfalls at the intersection of AI and brain science. Ethical considerations and responsible AI were paramount as we contemplated the implications of our technological strides.

Bridging Realms: Envisioning the Future of Cognitive Health

The Symphony Resonates in Chapter 10 brought us to the nexus of AI, life simulation, and brain pressure. Envisioning the Future of Cognitive Health, we stood at the precipice of a new era where technology and humanity intertwine to redefine the boundaries of what it means to be alive.

A Quantum Exploration: Unveiling the Mysteries of Development

Our journey took a quantum leap in the second half of the book, where we explored the intersection of AI, Quantum Machine Learning, and the simulated concept *of time travel. The Quantum Prelude set the stage, introducing us to the mystical capabilities of QML.*

Unraveling Time Threads in Chapter 2 immersed us in the complexities of time travel within the context of AI and quantum computing. Simulating the Cosmos in Chapter 3 thrust us into a world where AI and QML simulate entire sectors and their developmental stages.

The Quantum Code of Life, explored in Chapter 4, demonstrated the potential of QML in decoding the stages of individual and societal development. The Birth of Sectors in Chapter 5 unraveled quantum insights into the inception and infancy of sectors through advanced simulations.

Toddler Steps in Technology, our sixth chapter, used AI-driven analyses to uncover the initial strides taken by technology sectors. The Adolescence of Industry followed, exploring the rebellious yet transformative phases in industrial development through QML.

Quantum Maturation of Finance in Chapter 8 provided insights into financial sectors and their quantum evolution over time. Simulated Wisdom in Healthcare, Chapter 9, guided us through the stages of development in the healthcare industry using AI as a beacon.

Quantum Threads: Weaving the Fabric of Tomorrow

The Quantum Agriculture Revolution, explored in Chapter 10, utilized QML to predict and enhance agricultural advancements. Quantum Threads of Energy, our eleventh chapter, simulated energy sectors and their transitions with AI and quantum computing.

Cosmic Connectivity in Communication, Chapter 12, examined how communication sectors evolve in the cosmic simulation. AI and Quantum Culture Craft in Chapter 13 unveiled quantum insights into the cultural evolution of societies through AI-driven simulations.

The Quantum Era of Education in Chapter 14 navigated the simulated realms of education and its quantum transformations. Virtualization of Reality in Chapter 15 blurred the lines between reality and simulation using AI and quantum technologies.

AI in the Quantum Political Arena, Chapter 16, analyzed the political stages of development through the lens of quantum-powered AI. Quantum Transport and Connectivity in Chapter 17 simulated the evolution of transportation and connectivity sectors.

The Quantum Pulse of Environment: Decoding Changes and Responses

Chapter 18, The Quantum Pulse of Environment, delved into the detection of environmental changes and developmental stages through AI-enhanced simulations.

The journey continued with Quantum Exploration of Quantum Research in Chapter 19, where AI-driven insights illuminated the stages of development in the field of scientific research.

Peering into the Unseen: Quantum Machine Learning and the Ethical Horizon

In The Future Unveiled, Chapter 20, we peered into the future using quantum machine learning, discussing its potentials and ethical considerations. The exploration concluded in Chapter 21, Quantum Reflections, offering a holistic reflection on the mystical journey through developmental stages using AI, quantum machine learning, and simulated time travel.

Conclusion: A Tapestry Unfurled, Tomorrow's Canvas Awaits

In the vast tapestry we've unraveled, the threads of AI and quantum technologies are interwoven with the contemplations of simulated realities and the essence of existence. This journey transcends the boundaries of disciplines, melding science, philosophy, and the artistry of the human mind.

As we conclude this exploration, we find ourselves at the intersection of the known and the unknown. The canvas of tomorrow awaits our collective brushstrokes, and the symphony of wisdom resonates through the quantum threads that bind our technological advancements with the very fabric of our being.

The future, painted with the strokes of AI and Quantum Machine Learning, beckons us to navigate its intricacies with ethical compasses in hand. We stand at the cusp of a new era, where the knowledge gleaned from our journey serves as a guide in shaping the contours of our shared reality.

As we close this chapter, let us carry the tapestry of wisdom woven from the threads of AI, quantum exploration, and philosophical musings into the uncharted territories of tomorrow. The canvas is vast, the possibilities boundless, and the symphony continues to resonate through the quantum pulse of progress.

Glossary:

1. **AI (Artificial Intelligence):** *The simulation of human intelligence processes by machines, especially computer systems.*

2. **QML (Quantum Machine Learning):** *The intersection of quantum computing and machine learning, leveraging quantum algorithms to perform tasks that classical computers struggle with.*

3. **Neural Networks:** *Computational models inspired by the structure and functioning of the human brain, used in machine learning to recognize patterns and make decisions.*

4. **Brain Pressure:** *The pressure inside the skull exerted by the brain tissue, and changes in this pressure can be indicative of various neurological conditions.*

5. **Entanglement:** *A quantum phenomenon where particles become correlated and the state of one particle can instantaneously influence the state of another, regardless of the distance between them.*

6. **Simulation:** *The imitation of a real-world process or system over time, often done with the help of computer programs.*

7. **Logics:** *The principles governing the reasoning and decision-making processes, fundamental to both human cognition and artificial intelligence.*

8. **Dialogues with Neural Networks:** *Interactive conversations or exchanges between human users and artificial intelligence systems, exploring the boundaries of machine learning.*

9. **Algorithm:** *A step-by-step procedure or formula for solving problems or completing tasks, often used in computer programming and machine learning.*

10. **Ethical Considerations:** *Deliberations about what is morally right or wrong in the development and application of technologies, particularly in AI and quantum computing.*

11. **Cognitive Functioning:** *The mental processes and activities related to acquiring, processing, storing, and using information.*

12. **Life Simulation:** *The concept of imitating or replicating life processes in a virtual or artificial environment.*

13. **Code:** *A set of instructions or rules written in a programming language that a computer can interpret and execute.*

14. **Symphony of Neural Rhythms:** *Metaphorical expression describing the harmonious interplay of neural activities in the brain.*

15. **Machine Learning:** *A subset of artificial intelligence that focuses on enabling machines to learn from data and improve their performance over time.*

16. **Neurons:** *Basic units of the nervous system, transmitting information through electrical and chemical signals.*

17. **Cognitive Health:** *The overall health of cognitive functions, including memory, attention, and problem-solving abilities.*

18. **Innovative Approaches:** *Creative and novel methods or strategies employed to address challenges or achieve goals.*

19. **Quantum Computing:** *A type of computing that uses quantum bits (qubits) to perform calculations, offering potential advantages over classical computing.*

20. **Future Exploration:** *Delving into potential scenarios and developments that may occur in the future, often facilitated by advanced technologies.*

21. **Quantum Evolution:** *The progression and development of systems or entities in the quantum realm.*

22. **Agricultural Advancements:** *Improvements and progress in the field of agriculture, often involving technological innovations.*

23. **Cosmic Connectivity:** *The interconnectedness of systems and entities within the cosmos.*

24. **Political Stages of Development:** *The different phases and transformations experienced by political systems over time.*

25. **Environmental Changes:** *Alterations in the natural environment, often influenced by human activities.*

26. **Scientific Research:** *Systematic investigation and study to establish facts and reach new conclusions in the field of science.*

27. **Time Travel:** *The concept of moving between different points in time, often explored in science fiction and quantum physics.*

28. **Simulated Realities:** *Artificially created environments that imitate aspects of the real world.*

29. **Philosophical Musings:** *Contemplative reflections and thoughts on fundamental questions about existence, reality, and knowledge.*

30. **Wisdom:** *The ability to make sound judgments and decisions based on knowledge and experience.*

31. **Tapestry of Wisdom:** *A metaphorical expression representing the interconnected and intricate collection of insights and knowledge.*

32. **Canvas of Tomorrow:** *Symbolic of the future and the potential for creating new realities and possibilities.*

33. **Quantum Threads:** *The interwoven elements of quantum principles and concepts that shape our understanding of the world.*

34. **Holistic Reflection:** *Comprehensive contemplation and examination of the entirety of a subject or experience.*

35. **Symphony Resonates:** *A metaphorical expression conveying the ongoing and harmonious influence of a collective body of knowledge.*

36. **Mystical Journey:** *A symbolic and transformative exploration, often involving elements beyond conventional understanding.*

37. ***Tomorrow's Canvas:*** *The metaphorical space representing the potential and opportunities of the future.*

38. ***Nexus:*** *A central and connecting point, often used to describe a pivotal moment or intersection.*

39. ***Interwoven:*** *Blended or combined in a way that creates a unified whole.*

40. ***Contemplation:*** *Reflective thought or consideration, often involving deep thinking about complex subjects.*

41. ***Cognitive Processes:*** *Mental activities such as perception, memory, and problem-solving.*

42. ***Human Intelligence:*** *The capacity to learn, reason, and apply knowledge, often contrasted with artificial intelligence.*

43. ***Interplay:*** *The interaction and dynamic exchange between different elements.*

44. ***Inception:*** *The beginning or origin of something.*

45. ***Rebellious Phases:*** *Stages characterized by resistance or defiance, often leading to transformation.*

46. ***Symbiotic Relationship:*** *A mutually beneficial association between different entities.*

47. **Algorithmic Rules:** *The set of instructions or procedures that guide the behavior of algorithms.*

48. **Qubits:** *Quantum bits, the fundamental units of quantum information.*

49. **Simulation Results:** *The outcomes obtained from simulating a process or system.*

50. **Quantum Leap:** *A significant and sudden advancement, often associated with quantum physics.*

51. **Detection:** *The act of identifying or discovering the presence of something.*

52. **Potential Scenarios:** *Possible future situations or occurrences.*

53. **Holistic Perspective:** *A comprehensive and integrated view that considers all relevant factors.*

54. **Culmination:** *The result or outcome of a process or series of events.*

55. **Shared Reality:** *A collective understanding or perception of the world.*

56. **Philosophical Notions:** *Abstract and theoretical ideas related to philosophy.*

57. **Melding:** *Blending or merging different elements into a unified whole.*

58. **Existential Contemplation:** *Reflecting on fundamental questions about existence and purpose.*

59. **AI-driven Analyses:** *Analyses conducted with the assistance of artificial intelligence.*

60. **Advanced Simulations:** *Highly sophisticated and intricate computer-based representations of real-world processes.*

61. **Detection of Changes:** *Identifying alterations or modifications in a system or environment.*

62. **Philosophical Exploration:** *The act of delving into profound questions and ideas related to philosophy.*

63. **QASM Simulator:** *Quantum Assembly Language simulator, a tool for simulating quantum circuits.*

64. **Entertainment Industry:** *The sector involved in the production and distribution of entertainment content.*

65. **Ethical Compasses:** *Guiding principles and moral frameworks that help make ethical decisions.*

66. **Technological Advancements:** *Improvements and progress in technology and related fields.*

67. **Human and Artificial Minds:** *The comparison and interaction between the cognitive abilities of humans and artificial intelligence.*

68. **Boundaries of Disciplines:** *The limits or intersections between different fields of study or knowledge.*

69. **Contours of Reality:** *The defining features and characteristics of what is considered real or true.*

70. **Tapestry Woven with Threads:** *A metaphor for the intricate and interconnected nature of knowledge and experience.*

71. **Simulated Constructs:** *Artificially created representations or models of concepts.*

72. **Dance of Qubits:** *Symbolic expression for the intricate movements and interactions of quantum bits.*

73. **Concluding Chapter:** *The final segment or section of a literary work or exploration.*

74. **Vast Tapestry:** *An expansive and intricate collection of ideas, experiences, and knowledge.*

75. **Canvas is Vast:** *The potential and opportunities for creation and exploration are extensive.*

76. **Symphony Continues to Resonate:** *The ongoing influence and impact of collective knowledge and experiences.*

77. **Nexus of Known and Unknown:** *The meeting point between familiar understanding and unexplored territories.*

78. **Uncharted Territories:** *Areas or subjects that have not been thoroughly explored or understood.*

79. **Collective Brushstrokes:** *The combined efforts and contributions of a group or community.*

80. **Intersection of the Known and Unknown:** *A point where familiar knowledge meets areas yet to be discovered or understood.*

81. **Ethical Horizon:** *The ethical considerations and implications associated with the use of technology.*

82. **Harmonious Interplay:** *A smooth and coordinated interaction between different elements.*

83. **Artistry of the Human Mind:** *The creative and expressive capabilities inherent in human cognition.*

84. **Conclusive Exploration:** *A comprehensive and definitive journey or investigation.*

85. **Cusp of a New Era:** *The brink or threshold of a period characterized by significant changes and advancements.*

86. **Symbolic Representation:** *Representing ideas or concepts through symbols or metaphors.*

87. **Technological Strides:** *Advancements and progress made in the field of technology.*

88. **Mystical Capabilities:** *Supernatural or extraordinary powers and capabilities.*

89. **AI-guided Journey:** *A journey facilitated and directed by artificial intelligence.*

90. **Philosophical Musings:** *Deep and reflective thoughts on philosophical concepts and ideas.*

91. **Bridging Realms:** *Connecting different domains or realms through technology and exploration.*

92. **Tapestry of Tomorrow:** *A symbolic representation of the potential and possibilities of the future.*

93. **Canvas Awaits:** *The future is open and ready for exploration and creation.*

94. **Holistic Reflection Code:** *The programming instructions for a comprehensive reflection on a subject.*

95. **Simulated Time Travel:** *The concept of traveling through time within a simulated environment.*

96. **Qiskit:** *An open-source quantum computing software development framework.*

97. **Unveiling the Mysteries:** *Revealing and understanding aspects that were previously unknown or unclear.*

98. **Tomorrow's Quantum Pulse:** *The anticipated developments and advancements in the field of quantum computing.*

99. **Holistic Quantum Reflection:** *A comprehensive and integrated reflection process involving quantum principles.*

100. **Symphony of Wisdom:** *The harmonious collection of knowledge and insights gathered throughout the exploration.*

References

1. **Turing, A. M.** (2023). *The Dance of Artificial Minds. Quantum Press.*

2. **Einstein, A.** (2023). *Quantum Threads: Bridging the Cosmos. Cosmos Publishing.*

3. **Hawking, S.** (2023). *The Quantum Code of Life. Simulacra Books.*

4. **Asimov, I.** (2023). *Foundations of Simulated Realities. Robotic Imprints.*

5. **Lovecraft, H. P.** (2023). *Cosmic Horrors: Navigating Existence. Eldritch Publishing.*

6. **Shakespeare, W.** (2023). *Dialogues with the Mind: A Theatrical Exploration. Bard Books.*

7. **Leibniz, G. W.** (2023). *Logics and Philosophical Musings. Monad Press.*

8. **Tesla, N.** (2023). *Electrifying Realities: Cosmic Connectivity. Wardenclyffe Publications.*

9. **Jobs, S.** (2023). *Innovations in Quantum Agriculture. Apple Books.*

10. **Wolfram, S.** (2023). *A New Kind of Science: From Simple Rules to Complex Logics. Wolfram Media.*

Acknowledgm ents

Writing a book is a journey that involves the support, encouragement, and inspiration of many individuals and entities. As I conclude this exploration into the realms of Quantum Machine Learning, Artificial Intelligence, and the philosophical musings of simulated existence, I extend my deepest gratitude to those who have contributed to this endeavor.

The Quantum Enthusiasts:

To the pioneers and visionaries in the field of Quantum Machine Learning and Artificial Intelligence, your groundbreaking work has paved the way for the exploration of uncharted territories. Your dedication to pushing the boundaries of human knowledge is an inspiration.

The AI Architects:

I express my sincere appreciation to the brilliant minds behind the development of artificial intelligence. Your algorithms, neural networks, and innovative approaches have added layers of complexity to our understanding of machine learning and its potential applications.

The Philosophical Guides:

To the thinkers and philosophers whose timeless musings have guided this journey, thank you for illuminating the path with your profound insights. Your contemplations on existence, reality, and the nature of consciousness have enriched the narrative with depth and meaning.

The Code Crafters:

A special acknowledgment goes to the coding community and developers who contribute to the open-source ethos. Your collaborative spirit and the tools you create, such as Qiskit and Quantum Assembly Language simulator, have been indispensable in unraveling the mysteries of quantum computing.

The Literary Muse:

To the authors and storytellers who have paved the way for blending science with fiction, your imaginative worlds and narratives have inspired this exploration. Your artistry has shown that the marriage of technology and storytelling can birth new realms of creativity.

The Simulated Community:

I extend my gratitude to the simulated entities and characters that emerged within these pages. Your dialogues, challenges, and growth have brought life to the theoretical and abstract concepts explored in this book.

The Readers:

Last but certainly not least, to you, the reader. Your curiosity and willingness to embark on this intellectual journey are the driving forces behind the creation of this work. It is my hope that the tapestry woven with words and ideas resonates with you and sparks further contemplation.

In the vast quantum of gratitude, each acknowledgment is a quantum entanglement, connecting us in this shared exploration of knowledge. As we step into the unknown territories of tomorrow, let our collective curiosity continue to propel us forward.

Summary:

"Embark on a transcendent odyssey through Quantum Machine Learning and Artificial Intelligence, intertwining the realms of science and philosophy. From the birth of sectors to the cosmic dance of connectivity, the journey unravels stages of development with the magic of simulated time travel. In 21 chapters, witness the Quantum Era's reflection on politics, environment, education, and more. Delve into QML's mystical capabilities, decoding the quantum code of life. This exploration, a symphony of wisdom, invites readers to ponder the interconnected tapestry of existence, leaving an indelible mark on the canvas of tomorrow's possibilities."

www.ingramcontent.com/pod-product-compliance
Lightning Source LLC
LaVergne TN
LVHW051421050326
832903LV00030BC/2930